Embodying the Power of the Zero Stress Zone

By Yogi Amrit Desai

Compiled and Edited by Peggy Sealfon

STONEWATER
STUDIO
BOOKS

Published in the United States by
Stonewater Studio Books, 8805 Tamiami Trail N #130, Naples, FL 34108
StonewaterStudioBooks.com

Names: Desai, Amrit. | Sealfon, Peggy, compiler, editor.
Title: Embodying the power of the Zero Stress Zone / by Yogi Amrit Desai ; compiled and edited by
Peggy Sealfon.
Description: First edition. | Naples, FL : Stonewater Studio Books, 2017.
Identifiers: LCCN 2016959383 | ISBN 978-0-9963666-2-5
Subjects: LCSH: Stress management. | Anxiety. | Peace of mind. | Consciousness. | Self-help
techniques. | Conduct of life.
Classification: LCC BL629.5.S77 D47 2017 | DDC 294.5442--dc23

ISBN: 978-0-996366-2-5

Dedication

This book is dedicated to you, the reader, who seeks change as personal growth and an expanded understanding of life. May you be empowered to utilize these wisdom teachings to transform your world.

Acknowledgments

To the many thousands of students worldwide who have been inspired by and inspire others through these teachings. To those who have personally experienced profound shifts and transformed their lives through the practice of the Integrative Amrit Method (I AM) at the Amrit Yoga Institute. Very special thanks to those individuals who contributed to these pages by sharing their personal stories.

With appreciation to Lila Ivey and the late Diane Hanson for their feedback and support that contributed to the evolution of this book. Limitless gratitude to Deb Blish who provided a perpetual flow of information, review, and reflection that continually improved the content and structure of this book.

Table of Contents

Being Stress-Free Is Attainable
What Is I AM?
Internal Connection & Relaxation
Unconscious Causes of Stress
Prevention and the Truth About Illness
New Hope

Chronic Stress Is Hazardous to Your Health
Disconnecting From Feeling
Discovering Who You Are
Examining Patterns of Illusions

The Divine Conflict
You Create Your Own Reality
The Vital Role of Life Force
The Energy of Life
Your Shadow Self and the Button Pusher
A Key Concept: "Energy Follows Attention"
Capacity of Mind and Time
Wisdom of Prana—Freedom from Self-Caused Suffering
A Deeper Understanding: Going Beyond Limitations
Taking One Step

Finding the Self in the Present
The Self-Conscious Ego-Mind
The Seeds of the Past
Knowing Who You Are
Thoughts, Feelings, and Emotions Are Not Reality
Reactions In Disguise
The Button Pusher Is a Mirror
Presence Is Undivided
Choiceless Awareness Is the Solution to the Real Problem
Understanding Polarity and Duality

Preface

The Zero Stress Zone is a sacred place in which you can release all struggles and be united at last with who you are. Stress, anxiety, depression, and their manifestations—including self-limiting behaviors, fears, addictions, and disease—can be dissolved as rapidly as ice vanishes in hot water. You can solve life's conflicts by reconnecting to timeless truths that awaken an inner dimension: the essence of you.

Through the Integrative Amrit Method (I AM) techniques in this book, you are guided on a step-by-step voyage into an effortless zone of grace and profound contentment. The simplification of ancient approaches—of I AM Yoga—is revolutionary. The insights and clear experiences offer you a real and valuable chance to change forever what isn't working in your life and embrace vitality, happiness, and love in a sustainable way.

The unique feature of the I AM technique is that it goes beyond helping you release the energy trapped in your self-destructive habits and compulsive patterns;

it liberates energies from your stress-creating past. The system works at an inner, subtler level, restructuring the energetic frequency of your life energy and moving it into higher integrative levels. As you change your energetic frequency, you initiate changes in your energy centers.

Stress lives within but appears to be coming from everywhere, everything, and everyone. As you react, you perceive problems caused by outside elements or from another person. But these are illusions. They are recreations of stresses from unresolved memories in your past. If you are reacting and feeling conflict, only you can convert your reactive perception to responsive interaction and dismantle the stress that you are creating. The moment you convert your reaction into response, you transform conflict into harmony, tension into relaxation, separation into unification, and fears into compassion. These inner changes become the process of self-discovery that brings you progressively closer to the source of "I am" within. When you understand this transformative process of the Zero Stress Zone, it becomes accessible. It creates remarkable shifts internally. You will have the master key as you take back your power and transcend conflict and stress to enter a place of love, peace, and harmony within.

The most popular yoga of today is not yoga. Once an obscure and esoteric mystery, yoga has become common in recent decades by a growing interest in health and well-being. While offering a multitude of therapeutic and healing benefits, the ancient spiritual practice has been adapted to appeal to a contemporary mass market, and much of its core spirit has been lost. Yoga was never meant to be limited to a physical discipline restricted to *asanas* or postures. Yoga means "union," and its purpose is to awaken the integration of body, mind, and spirit, which is essential for balancing all life's forces.

Yoga is life. Whether you realize it or not, you're practicing yoga when arguing with your spouse, children, or boss, or when you feel jealously, anger, resentment, or fear. These are postures. You also practice yoga when you are in a loving embrace, starting a new job, moving to a new home, becoming a new parent, or even singing a beautiful tune. Who you are and how you interact with life experiences is what the practice of yoga makes clearer to you.

Why is this important for you to know? You'll want to understand that what you are about to read and experience within these pages is a more direct and deeper route to relieve human suffering. It is a powerful way to discover unity, self-actualization, and joy. You will be guided to embody the power of the Zero Stress Zone that is uniquely available through the I AM techniques.

The approaches provide an intentional practice for aligning body, mind, and spirit using a Posture of Consciousness. Consciousness is a state of accepting, without resistance, all that is present within the range of physical, mental, and emotional experiences at any given moment. You'll be enabled to descend from the form of thinking and doing through feeling to the non-doing power of being, of presence.

You will learn how your thoughts are subtle forms that are created from the ego-mind. Your being is form-less. Your body is where you embody the being that you are, and the connection to the body is through feeling. You cannot connect to the inner formless dimension of your true divine potential through the mind. When you try, you confront stress, frustrations, and unhealthy imbalances.

If you have an angry thought, for example, that negative impulse connects to the subconscious, activating glands that release toxic chemicals in the body. To change to a positive connection and alter the harmful effects, you must disengage from the mind so the sympathetic nervous system restores balance in the body, signaling the immune system to function efficiently and to renew health and harmony.

It is not unusual to become a slave of your own mind. When the mind acts unconsciously from acquired habits and past conditionings, you experience fear, anger, hatred, blame, shame, or guilt. Your vital life force diminishes. Any "doing" carried out by the ego-mind engages in comparison, criticism, judgment and competition. Through these pages, you will be shown how to develop your mind to unfold your human and spiritual potential in a way that leads to a fulfilling experience of life.

The practices in this book explain how to turn the light of witnessing presence into a self-discovery process using a one-step solution. In this way, you can intentionally withdraw from reactions that dominate your life force and compromise the wisdom of your body. Through posture of consciousness, you'll cultivate the ability to see the truth and transition from unreality to reality and from time bound ego-mind to the timeless power of presence. This path can profoundly change your life.

The inherent values of the I AM techniques (including Amrit Yoga, Yoga Nidra, and Quantum Breath Meditation) allow you to reveal and accept your spirit-driven purpose. Each step is an opportunity to release (1) fear of failure or success or (2) a need to be anyone other than how you experience yourself in this moment and from moment to moment. It is an opportunity to transform any blockages and limitations in your physical, mental, and emotional bodies so that you may realize your expansive potential and live blissfully in the Zero Stress Zone, beyond time and space. To enter it, you have to let go of the reactive perceiver that lives in the dimension of time and is the fundamental cause of all conflicts and stress that appear in your body-mind.

You have been guided to this book for a reason. You will benefit in infinite ways and integrate with your true self. By changing yourself, you have the potential to transform your world into heaven on earth.

Foreword

I believe in synchronicity. An odd sequence of
events aligned to bring me to my first weekend workshop with Gurudev Amrit Desai (*Shri Amritji*) in
Tampa, Florida. I was one of 200 people who came
to learn from this world-renowned Yogi Master,
founder of Kripalu Center of Yoga & Holistic Health
in Massachusetts. Dressed in traditional, long, white
embroidered Kurta, Gurudev glided onto the stage, his
silver-streaked hair flowing in loose cascades around
his narrow, chiseled face, which had an angelic glow. As
his Indian-accented words floated out to me, his energy
and enthusiasm were contagious and his delivery,
humorous and disarming.

I had an uncanny sense that he was speaking only
to me and that no one else existed in the room—a
highly unusual sensation that, I found out later, was
shared by most of the other participants. Everything
Gurudev said—pure, clear teachings—resonated deep
within me, creating a continual series of "a-ha" mo-

ments. He shared techniques that connected me to a sense of myself I had long forgotten.

About five months later, I attended another workshop, this time at the Amrit Yoga Institute in Salt Springs, Florida, which is in the midst of the Ocala National Forest, nestled alongside Lake Kerr. By the end of the two-day program, I felt amazingly calm and happy. Instead of being a bundle of fractured energy, I felt centered and quiet; my energies integrated, full of purpose and direction. Everyone around me was feeling joyful, and we bonded together in this ocean of loving energy. In talking to Gurudev's son, Malay, I heard myself offer to help reach more people who could benefit from Gurudev's teachings. (At the time, I owned an advertising agency.) Suddenly, I was in Gurudev's house, sharing ideas with the master himself. The process seemed ethereal and dreamlike. I did not have any inkling that that meeting would change my life forever.

Synchronicity continued to be at play. Fast-forward to eight months later; I was sponsoring a weekend with Yogi Desai in Naples, Florida, tied in with a fundraiser which drew more than 350 attendees. In a follow-up meeting, Gurudev told me: "You should be trained and teach." I was surprised, as I thought to myself: I'm a marketing professional, a journalist, a writer. "You are a teacher," Gurudev insisted. "A Yogini. Do a meditation class." I listened. I went on to become certified in Yoga Nidra, then Amrit Yoga and beyond.

This book is the fruition of an intention to disseminate information about transformational opportunities that were catalysts for monumental change in my own life, and I've witnessed how they have touched so many. The format is a presentation of stress-reducing methods, along with deep philosophical understanding of ancient teachings assembled from a multitude of Gurudev's writings, articles, and discourses (darshans). The focus has been primarily on organizing his work in a way that reveals its inner depth more fully.

Often, spiritual practitioners attempt to teach the secret of life—of cultivating the ability to enter the present moment—through a major jump from thinking to being. Such a massive shift from form to formless can be too wide a chasm to navigate successfully in today's high-intensity lifestyles. In this book, you will learn a sequential unfolding, from thinking to feeling to being. Gurudev's breakthrough approach, passed down through his lineage, is far more adaptable and accessible for anyone to activate rapid change in today's tumultuous lifestyles than anything currently available.

To enter the Zero Stress Zone, you'll access an eso-teric world of sacred teachings in which you'll become more directly connected to an understanding of the truth of existence. These ancient practices, attained by honored yogis and sages thousands of years ago, are demystified and explained by Gurudev in an approach-able way, so that you can apply them practically in your everyday life.

In the process of compiling the book, Gurudev met with me every month or so to review chapters and refine them to reflect a clearer communication. Sometimes while working together, we would co-create concepts based on his original works; other times. I realized it was to deepen my understanding to enhance my abilities to communicate them. To make the in-formation more relevant, I interviewed students who have been transformed by Gurudev's teachings. I have included a few of their stories and experiences through-out the book for heightened insights and enjoyment.

My own major breakthrough was the recognition that I no longer had to live life on an extreme see-saw of manic highs and lows. Through the practice of this work, I've entered a neutral state where I remain perpetually content, productive, and healthy.

My life mission has become focused on helping others connect to their own source to expand inner skills and supercharge their lives. As a personal development coach, author, and motivational speaker, I'm gratified to have opportunities to share transformational tools to effect positive change. In reaching my own increased levels of awareness, I've embraced a loving intimate relationship with a caring man that reaffirms the mysterious ways of walking the walk ... and I continue to learn.

My intention through this project has been to honor and respect Gurudev's teachings, as he is the carrier of the energetic flow of his lineage to Swami Sri Kripalvanandji (also called Swami Kripalu) and Lord Lakulisha (known as Dadaji). It is to shine a beacon on ancient methods as guiding lights for many to navigate and transcend challenges, fears, and frustrations of our ever-changing modern world. I feel deeply privileged to have had so many hours upon hours of time to spend with Gurudev to explore, ask questions, reflect on the essence of the work, and experience and observe my own continual growth. After several years of working on this project, I'd arrive at the next session confident that the book was now complete. But then, as we reviewed chapters together, Gurudev—in his own inimitable journey of transformation—would have more insights and a new level of clarity that would send me back for revisions. The process continually enhanced and expanded communication of the essence of the work.

I'm humbled to offer the book as a culmination of this process and a reflection of more than 55 years of Gurudev's commitment to living within the spirit of his ancestors and sharing his deep perceptions in a way that make them accessible for all of us. May you find within these pages the gateway for yourself to discover your path to personal purpose, good health, fulfillment, and happiness. *Jai Bhagwan.*

Peggy Sealfon
January 2, 2017

Introduction

Being Stress-Free Is Attainable

As you learn to enter into the innermost core of an integrative state of being, complications in life dissolve along with conflicts that cause anxiety, depression, frustration, or fear. You'll mindfully recognize many different ways that your energy gets abusively and self-destructively used up in your current patterns and how it affects your health, relationships, perception of happiness, and your entire life. You'll learn one-step turnaround techniques instead of thousands of fruitless steps that lead you down dead-end roads. As you embark on a path of changing yourself, you will be amazed as the whole world changes with you. The Zero Stress Zone will expand your perceptions and create: openings, where there was closure; understanding, where there were doubt and confusion; and communication, where there were miscommunication and conflict. The penetrating and insightful teachings will provide you with an understanding of the mind-body-spirit connection in a way that can be practically and usefully assimilated into your everyday life.

The moment you allow yourself to step out of your own limiting self-concepts, fears, and insecurities, you'll clearly see beyond the boundaries that hold you captive. Insights, intuition, and creativity will begin to bloom. The more you explore this dimension, the more you'll see and experience the miracles of being in the Zero Stress Zone.

Entering the Zero Stress Zone happens naturally at fleeting moments in life. Have you ever gotten so absorbed in a task that captured your total attention so fully that hours flew by, without your awareness of time passing? When you enter the Zone, everything you are doing becomes effortless, invigorating, and fulfilling. The sense of time is suspended, and the moment feels dreamlike—almost ethereal—with everything flowing smoothly and effortlessly. Athletes, dancers, artists, writers, and performers enter the Zone unconsciously after years of repetitive practice and training. They totally merge into the performance and enter the Zone, where time and effort totally disappear. The doer or performer disappears into the doing—into the performance—and miracles happen.

The Integrative Amrit Method (I AM) techniques are not about cultivating the technique but about connecting to the consciousness itself, so that you can enter the Zone consciously, regardless of what you are doing. In fact, you do not even need to be performing. In the former scenario of an artist or athlete, once the competition or performance is over, so is the feeling of communion. The mind resumes control, and the ego reenters into managing and controlling, which disconnects you from that effortless feeling, from the integration of mind and body. Many creative people whose livelihoods rely on their talents fear that the muse will simply disappear one day, and they will no longer be able to perform, write, or create. They have little understanding of how they got into the Zone or how to stay there.

Once you learn how to connect to the source within, you can enter the Zone regardless of where you are, what you are doing, or whom you are with. It goes with you everywhere, always available. When you are cultivating a skill, you are changing only one part of the whole that you are, but when you cultivate the consciousness, which is the source of everything you do, it begins to illuminate every expression and every aspect of your life—turning your life into a stress-free flow. It is about embodying the experience of oneness.

What Is I AM?

The I AM yoga is wrapped around an integrated yoga that was first introduced to North America in the 1960s by Yogi Desai. The true meaning and direct experience of yoga is "union," uniting mind, body, heart, and spirit into one—something often missing from or completely misunderstood in the popular practice of yoga today. Many practitioners do not delve into the depths that will be revealed on these pages. Often, the focus is only on the forms and the postures/asanas. There is so much more that can bring you effortlessly into the Zone. Many yoga students, as well as many people seeking a better, more fulfilling life, neglect aspects that are essential for growth, longevity, and health. Discovering these essentials is the unique aspect of the I AM yoga, which provides a gateway for redesigning your destiny. The opportunity is available to anyone at any age and at any level of fitness, consciousness, and understanding. The only requirements are an open mind, an open heart, and a willingness to explore and experiment—because this dimension is beyond traditional understanding.

Internal Connection and Relaxation

The Zero Stress Zone is a deeply integrated state of being, where you recognize that the source of power and healing is hidden within you. It is contained in the internal part of yourself that can be achieved consciously through deep relaxation. Yogis have known how to enter this innate state of unity with ease and how the Zone is accessible at any time, even in the midst of chaos.

Many of the currently accepted types of relaxation are shallow and superficial. After a day's hard work, many people turn on television, play music, go out for dinner, have a drink, dance, or engage in some recreational activity. Each serves only as a distraction from the original tension. Distractions do not provide deep relaxation; they only conceal tension temporarily, rather than resolving it at the source.

For instance, exercise is often used for relaxation. Sports, gym workouts, walking, yoga, and pilates help reduce tension—but they release physical tensions only from the surface, not from the cause or the root. Of course, physical exercise obviously increases muscle activity, circulation, and respiration, so there are benefits—but these are fleeting.

Let's say you've exercised for two hours. You feel good, and you go out for a drive. You get cut off by another driver, and, instantly, you're upset and angry. Exercise provides only temporary relief that doesn't carry over into other tensions that arise throughout the day. Instead, if you learn how to connect to your inner source of strength and power, you avoid getting caught in emotional, stress-producing, and conflict-creating emotional reactions.

Unconscious Causes of Stress

Through exercise, you can relax the body using physical forms. This does not cultivate consciousness or true awareness; rather, it cultivates only the body. The truth is that the source of tension lies hidden in the unconscious, which feeds problems that appear on the surface as conflicts and reactions. In these pages, you will learn how to develop an internal awareness to let go of all blockages and holdings.

Medical journals and scientific studies have proven, over and over, that physical, mental, and emotional illnesses are stress-related. According to a May 1991 article in **USA Magazine** cited by the American Institute of Stress, "...75 - 90 percent of all visits to primary care physicians are for stress related problems." It explains that many of the effects of stress "are due to increased sympathetic nervous system activity and an outpouring of adrenaline, cortisol and other stress-related hormones." Stress is an epidemic, and many accept it as normal—but it takes a staggering toll on the health and productivity of the population.

Stress is a hidden cause, and illnesses appear as symptoms on the surface. To reach the core of the cause that lies hidden in your unconscious, you need methods that promote internal awareness and integration. Too often, your energy reserve, which is your principle investment, gets used up on behavioral habit patterns that offer no interest and cause you to lose your principle. Chronic stimulation of the sympathetic nervous system results in adrenal burnout and illness. You are about to discover a recipe for longevity by maintaining good health and homeostatic balance in your body and happiness through a deeply fulfilling and inner connection to your life energies. This approach will reveal to you that everything you truly want in your life is attainable, and you will learn exactly how to access the light of a new reality.

Prevention and the Truth About Illness

Self-abusive behaviors and habits deplete your energy and often result in obvious symptoms of "disease," leading to illness or injury. Prevention of these symptoms can prevent premature aging and improve quality of life. Any health-related exercises and activities, such as sports, dance, or yoga, can be taken to a whole new level by applying the methodologies in this book. By incorporating these strategies into your daily life, your life experiences become transformational. You'll realize you already have what you need and can forgo any kind of esoteric journey to the top of a spiritual mountain. With practice, you will notice changes in your life that will reflect in your health, intimate relationships, work, and more. Within weeks, you may recognize huge shifts in how you approach both challenges and opportunities in your life. In fact, perceived challenges may transform into opportunities!

The website Mercola.com cites the American Medical Association as stating that "80% of all health problems are stress related." Therefore, the real secret to good health and longevity is simply to stay mentally and emotionally balanced, without spikes of highs and lows. But it is not always so clear. Let's accept that physical illness is based upon a cause hidden deep in the unconscious. *Symptoms that appear on the surface are effects. Treat the cause in the unconscious and the symptoms will disappear. Treat the symptoms and the cause will reappear in other forms.*

The Western approach to healthcare is focused on treating symptoms. Instant fixes of pharmaceuticals or surgical procedures have become an accepted norm. Often, these methods do not resolve the cause and may treat just one part of the imbalance. They may make you feel better in the short term but may not have long-lasting curative effects; they may even create additional side effects. Of course, if you have an acute illness or a physical problem that requires medical intervention, medical approaches are necessary options. However, after and during treatments, these methods can hasten the recuperation period and promote healing and recovery. These techniques can be used in cooperation with traditional drugs and other complementary medicine. Most importantly, the techniques can be used as a preventative, to keep the body balanced and boost the immune system to ward off illnesses of all kinds. Prevention needs to become an integral part of cultural orientation, as it is essential for long-term survival.

Prevention can begin with experiencing the inner dimension that removes symptoms from the source and restores balance to your body, mind, and emotions. For instance, if you are suffering from stress precipitated from a divorce, severe illness, or the death of a loved one, you can learn to silence the disturbances and restlessness of the mind. As you move closer to the source, the center, you become more progressively relaxed, and your mind becomes more peaceful, more connected to an almost childlike place within. That's when you find yourself in the Zero Stress Zone, entering through a most unique path.

Here you experience that part of yourself that is always present but hidden from your awareness. In this Zone, you tap into objective, clear perceptions that reveal solutions, where before you saw only problems. You rise above past memories and habits and consciously cross over into the limitless, expansive zone of spirit. Emotional stress, trauma, and hurts are dismantled and released spontaneously, effortlessly, and automatically.

Imagine stepping into a state of being where all boundaries of body and mind dissolve. Freed from the inhibitions of mind and time, you rest in the boundless space of your being. The power of the I AM yoga interrupts reactive patterns and directs life energy to relieve pain, refresh your mind, and revitalize your body.

New Hope

A student in Naples, Florida, called the experience of learning the I AM techniques her "new awareness." She said:

> "The ability to enter inner quiet and peace at a time in my life that is full of fear and anxiety ... I feel more able to live in the moment and allow and experience childlike happiness, regardless of significant fear and anxiety in my life. It can be separate from me. I'm so grateful for these techniques. They are all the more powerful because I wouldn't have believed I could have moments of perfect peace at this time in my life. I have new hope. These were moments of peace and quiet that I have sought and not found for more than a year. I have a beginning now, not an end."
> —N.P., Naples, Florida

Chapter 1

Entering the Zero Stress Zone

Chronic stress is dangerous. It keeps the body functioning at a high alert level that drains the immune system and weakens organs, ultimately resulting in illnesses that range from cancers to fibromyalgia and from diabetes to strokes and heart attacks. Work, food, sex, and drugs are used as antidotes. Instead of eliminating stress, they further induce it. Anxiety, fear, and frustration caused by stress disrupt family life, love life, and professional life. Stress creates dysfunction and causes misery by taking away the freedom to be happy, creative, efficient, and effective. It takes you further from the Zone.

Chronic Stress Is Hazardous to Your Health

Stress is insidious. Activated from the survival mechanism known as the "fight or flight" instinct, it has been honed through human evolution to prepare for survival against hostile primitive conditions and predators that constituted real threats to life. Modern-day stress is far different, triggered more by attacks of psychological threats to the self-image through the many different roles that people play in relationships as parents, children, employees, teachers, and spouses. It is created from reactions to family members, coworkers, and a variety of other external influences. Emotional reaction is identical to the instinctual fight-or-flight response and has the same physiological impact.

The body responds to these psychological elements by increasing the heart rate and raising blood pressure to increase the flow of blood to the brain, where the alarm goes off to flee from danger. The psychological danger is of your own making. It's a false alarm, arising from your reactions to what is present.

These automatic reactions arise in defense of survival of your self-image. They are in defense against an enemy that does not exist. Reactions merely arise out of preprogrammed, self-images that are inconsistent with the reality that is being faced in the moment. The attention and energy that fight with the nonexistent enemy are self-destructive as you fight a phantom self-image. You're battling an illusion.

Consider a 55-year-old man who is consumed with fear. The economy is poor, and he's afraid of losing his job. He's panicked about not being good enough to get another job at his age and not having enough money for his family and his future. Yet, in the reality of the moment, he has a job, a beautiful home, savings, and a healthy family, and his wife has an excellent job. Despite all of that, he is caught in a false fear. Why? When he was a young boy, his parents delivered a message that he'd never amount to anything, and the fear of losing his job has triggered an old pattern of denying his own self-worth. It isn't real. It's just an image from a long-ago past.

Chronic stress causes hypertension, stroke, heart attacks, diabetes, ulcers, body aches, and pains. Many of these effects are the result of relentless stimulation of the sympathetic nervous system, causing an outpouring of adrenaline, cortisol, and other stress-related hormones. Stress affects other hormones that regulate the metabolism, brain neurotransmitters, and more, which can further impair the immune system.

Disconnecting From Feeling

Stress affects body and mind. It is a fundamental cause of the loss of your ability to feel. When you are engaged by stress-producing activities on a mental and emotional level, you become insensitive to what is happening in your body. The more insensitive you get, the more you become disconnected from your energy body. Your energy becomes fractured and fragmented, and your mind becomes distracted and dysfunctional. Energy and attention are interconnected.

Once you are deprived of the capacity to feel, you lose touch with life-giving functions of your body. When you are very angry or jealous, you suddenly lose your appetite. You lose your sexual urges. You feel withdrawn from love, children, spouse, and friends. All of a sudden, your energy is blocked, and your connection with your heart center is disrupted. You cannot feel anything. You're out of touch with your health and well-being. It is important to understand that your fundamental connection to life and happiness is intrinsically tied to your ability to feel and perceive the reality of what is as it is.

When you're tense, you stop feeling to the point that you don't even know if you're hungry. If you do eat, you overeat, because you're not feeling sensations. You're not mindful. You're not present. You cannot even feel if you're satisfied. Your body says one thing, and your mind says another.

The chatter of the mind becomes overwhelming. Before you eat, you may be thinking you shouldn't eat too much, but while you're eating, you're disconnected from the feeling. Another voice in your mind says, "Go on, have a good time." You listen to the new thought and indulge in it. But when you finish, another voice comes up and says "Here you go again. You didn't listen, and you ate too much. You messed up again." What happened? You became absorbed in your crowded mind and disconnected from the sensitivity to your body, to your feeling center. Feeling is the voice of the body, and when you abuse it, it becomes dull.

As a result, your mind is overtaken by different voices that are not in synchronicity with the feeling of the body, of the life force energy, called *Prana*. This means that your self-conscious self-image and your energy body are living in conflict. The mind is dedicated to its preprogrammed habit patterns and continues to superimpose those patterns over the subconscious *Pranic* wisdom of the body. The mind is the master and carries out compulsive habit patterns.

The attention of animals is intimately tied to their biological urges. They lack the freedom to act differently from their inborn biological survival instincts for food, water, shelter, and procreation. These biological urges are shared by human beings. Human beings differ because individual choices allow people to override natural, biological urges. Instead, personal likes, desires, and fears flow from preconditioned self-image and influence people to act in certain ways that may not serve their well-being. People choose to avoid pain and seek pleasure. Some pain can be beneficial, though, such as hunger pains that alert people to fuel their bodies.

Feeling is a medium of direct connection of the energy body or *Prana*, to the soul. As a result, feeling becomes the direct and primary medium to experience life. As the victim of the unconscious, you progressively move further away from your connection to *Prana*. As that happens, you become weak and suffer blockages in the body, causing increased insensitivity. The neuro-glandular system that distributes secretions for healthy functioning is reduced. Life energy is depleted, and the immune system is compromised.

A practical explanation of energy can be made using cars as an example. If a car dropped from 6 horsepower to 1 horsepower, chances are good you would junk it. It would be ineffectual. This is precisely what happens in your body, where *Prana* represents the horsepower of the body. In another example, an electric fan rated to run on 220 volts but plugged into a 110-volt outlet clearly would be unable to perform efficiently. When the body is deprived of energy, it is progressively dysfunctional and susceptible to disease. When feeling deteriorates, your spirit diminishes, and you suffer more, experiencing fear, discomfort, pain, hurt, and exhaustion. You feel progressively less connected to all that you love. Your feeling center and your heart center are very intimately connected. If your feeling center is compromised, your love will be compromised. Your energy is running on empty.

Unconscious habit patterns and behaviors act as parasites that suck your life blood and leave you depleted of vital life force. When you are healthy, your capacities for thinking, feeling, and being are in perfect harmony. Your feeling is the center from which you can disengage from stress-producing physical and mental activity, so that everything you do comes from a feeling connected to the life force that is life-enhancing.

When you prevent your life force from being abusively used up and reinforce it with the methods in this book, you effectively eliminate the toxins and poisons from your body. Your survival-level instinctive connection to the subconscious body is much more alert, and fears based on your shadow images begin to disappear.

Instead, you find yourself in a place of pure love, with a pure mind and a healthy body that become more luminous and energetic.

Humans are born with an animal body, a human mind, and a divine potential. In human beings, there is an advanced level of evolution—an inborn sense of "I am" that functions as the self-conscious ego-mind and dominates your *Prana*, the subconscious energy body.

Discovering Who You Are

When you do not have a clear intention as to who you are, you get lost. No matter where you go, what you do, or who you are with, it gets you further away from who you really are. Whatever you are seeking from others or outside of yourself disconnects you from the feeling center, from the wisdom of the body that is the felt presence.

The use of feeling can return you to the connection to the body, acting as a link to the power of presence of the soul within. The body gives you the relation to the inner source. You look for something but don't know what it is you are looking for. Actions and reactions are driven by preprogrammed habits and behaviors that guide you into blind alleys with no way out. You've lost the connection to making mindful choices. The moment you can identify and know very clearly what it is that you want, you become united to the infinite source of power within, and everything else you want follows. The inner source is the ultimate destination that brings true and lasting joy and fulfillment, called *prosperity consciousness*. Prosperity cannot be measured by what you *have*—possessions—but by who you become in the process of getting what you have.

What you do to yourself to get what you want plays a significant role in entering prosperity consciousness. Most people ignore what they do to themselves because they're so exclusively guided by what they want from the external world or from another person in their lives. They cling to false concepts of prosperity that focus on one isolated part of life, which is purely external. Without being able to connect to the internal part of oneself, which is the ultimate destiny, all external destinations fail to provide the fulfillment of true prosperity consciousness.

Examining Patterns of Illusions

As revealed, stress appears on the surface in many different forms, through many different mediums, and seems as if it is coming from other people, life situations, and relationships that you face—but this is an illusion. It's like trying to find the moon in a lake where it appears in the form of a reflection or to touch the horizon where earth appears to meet the sky. Solving stress by changing people, places, and things exists like an elusive image until you understand that the cause lives within you. It remains inaccessible and invisible, becoming apparent only when it resurfaces as a reaction to who or what is present. That's the secret. That moment triggers old reactive memories that aren't real in the present. Once you know this, you can remove stress from its very cause that lives within you. Until then, you'll be groping to catch the moon in the lake or trying to fly faster to find the horizon line.

It's important to realize that the poisonous roots of all problems, conflicts, and stress—which appear to be coming from your love life, family life, work life, or social life—are hidden inside you. Consider the invisible roots of a tree, which can become visible in the form of poisonous plants and fruit on its branches. Even if you remove the external growths, the roots will recreate more toxic results. But if you remove the hidden roots, the poisonous flowers and fruits will automatically wither and die.

At first, it is challenging to accept that you are responsible for creating the conflicts in your life through your reactive perceptions influenced from the past. Your human nature as a *reactive perceiver* leads you to blame problems on external people or circumstances that trigger your reactions. You'll soon discover how to work internally and externally simultaneously. Only you have the ability to convert these reactive conflicts into responses. Your freedom of choice gives you the opportunity to dismantle stress from within, as well as stress from your external lifestyle, habits, or behavior patterns. You can take "response-ability" and choose your response rather than allow it to become an automatic reaction. When you realize that the reactive perceiver is already present within you, you'll accept that the other person or situation merely served as an association to trigger your reaction but was not the cause. Once you know this fact, you can create a paradigm shift of solving the problem from the source within you.

Remember, stress is not created by the other person; it is created by the way you react to the other person. With *every* reaction, you are potentially replaying an internal trauma, a painful experience, again and again. This is the chronic cause of stress, which appears to be coming from everywhere but which lives in the eye of the reactive perceiver, not the perceived.

The moment you convert your reaction into response, you transform conflict into harmony, tension into relaxation, separation into unification, and fears into compassion. These inner changes become the process of self-discovery that brings you progressively closer to the source within. Instead of targeting the illusive problem, you are going where the problem lives—inside—and turning reaction into response. Therefore, you dismantle the cause of stress—not just for that one occurrence but at the source within, to discontinue its reappearance. This will create remarkable internal shifts, transforming stress from agony of conflict, hurt, pain, and despair into harmony, health, and balance of the body, mind and beyond.

Internal resiliency—to respond to change without reaction—gives you the freedom to flow in life with what is. The change is imminent everywhere. As you learn to manage your response to the changing world of reality, you will be empowered.

Chapter 2

The Energy Body Empowers You

Energy flows with cosmic intelligence. It is the invisible cause seen visibly in the body. When you work with the resulting effects by going to the cause, you develop awareness of these subtle energies in the *Prana* of the energy body. You feel these energies and connect to the power within. The surface symptoms of depression, anxiety, fatigue, and insomnia, which often result from internal conflicts, can be released from the fundamental energy block that lies as a root cause. In this way, stress can be consciously dismantled. When you understand energetic anatomy, you will know the path to tapping into your inner healer, the innate wisdom of the body, and be able to live in the Zero Stress Zone.

Many people are unaware of how energy that feeds both the mind and body controls the health of the body and dramatically influences moods. Physical health and a clean body are the foundation for clearing the emotional body. Moods are the result of poisonous chemicals that create toxins and pollute the energy of the body. Releasing the trapped energy in the subconscious and karma body is fundamental in restoring health and spiritual development. Whenever subconscious energies are converted into the unconscious karma body, conditioned by the time-bound past of remembered experiences, the energies live in perpetual conflict with the superconscious cosmic body. Once you disconnect from your preprogrammed habit patterns, you will heal your body and function more optimally by releasing the subconscious energy trapped in the unconscious.

The conflict—between the individual ego-mind and the energy field of the individual body—causes stress. But this stress is more profound, as this conflict with the individual body is in conflict with the entire body of cosmic creation.

The Divine Conflict

The cosmic body of creation is composed of earth, water, fire, air, and ether. Your individual body is created of the same elements. When you live in perpetual conflict with your vital life force energy, your *Prana*, your capacity to absorb *Prana* through these five elements begins to diminish. The cosmic body of creation supplies all the *Prana*—the air, food, and water—but your deteriorating energy body cannot breathe the air or digest the food or water. You're no longer in tune with the ability to receive through the energy body. As a result, you suffer. Imbalances—such as indigestion, insomnia, fatigue, and other kinds of physical, mental, and emotional diseases—result from your living in perpetual conflict with the cosmic energy body that animates all creation as well as individual bodies. When you go against the creation, you go against the Creator. The Creator and his creation are inseparably one. A human being is born with an individual sense of ego-mind with a complete facility to create his or her own world by using the same energy as the cosmic "I am"—as you call God or the divine—to manifest through the cosmic body of creation.

You Create Your Own Reality

Each individual "I am" is born with an evolutionary gift to create his own world and shape it with his own thought forms. Unconscious actions manifest through the ego-mind arising out of the shadow or unconscious self-image that has separated from the Self, creating and shaping one's own individual world, one's karma.

Karma is the action that combines with thought and energy to create a new world of one's own imagination and perception that is totally inconsistent with the omnipresent presence of reality. For instance, consider five members of a family who are living in the same home, sharing the same lifestyle and foods—but each one creates his or her own independent perception of reality that may seem incompatible with the others. Each acts differently with varying likes, dislikes, and mood changes.

The Vital Role of Life Force

Most people do not recognize that they have two centers of perception: the center that deals with external, environmental life situations and the center of the superconscious, which is the infinite source of life force or *Pranic* energy. An essential skill for stress management is to understand the vital role that *Prana* plays as a powerful link among the different levels of your being. Breath is the medium through which *Prana*, the Holy Spirit, enters the body and animates all its life-giving functions. Circulation, digestion, elimination, and thousands of other subtle functions are simultaneously fed by *Prana* and carried by the breath. *Prana* also feeds and animates mental and emotional functions, activating the mind to function in the dimension of time. *Prana* feeds life. It animates the senses and is the medium of sensations and feelings. It is this *Prana* that carries out what are called involuntary functions in physiology.

Modern researchers are increasingly discovering the powerful healing impact of *Prana* and how to use it to treat health problems. Ancient sages, mystics, and yogis discovered the secrets of this life force that lies at the very core of one's being. They understood how the *Prana* body is an evolutionary GPS that can guide you at every step along the way. This powerful guidance system is infused with innate wisdom that leads you toward higher integrative centers of consciousness. They recognized that it is the universal intelligence that enters through the breath and remains as a divine potential within you. The purpose of the Integrated Amrit Method is to return back to that integrated source of being that is inborn within you and reconnect to the soul.

American Indians recognized this link. In an insightful Cherokee story, an old Cherokee told his grandson, "My son, there is a battle between two wolves inside us all. One is Evil. It is anger, jealousy, greed, resentment, inferiority, lies, and ego. The other is Good. It is joy, peace, love, hope, humility, kindness, empathy, and truth." The boy thought about it, and asked, "Grandfather, which wolf wins?" The old man quietly replied, "The one you feed."

The Energy of Life

> "By governing the force which governs the *Prana*, the Yogi can surround himself with the blaze of life."
> —Patanjali's Yoga sutra, chapter 2, verse 2:41

There is a distinct hierarchy of power that exists in the anatomy of being. The life of the senses is fed by *Prana*. A parable from the ancient scriptures of India vividly illustrates the importance of breath, of *Prana*. The parable is this: There was a large gathering of the five senses—sight, sound, touch, taste, smell—to decide who was the supreme ruler. In the gathering, each sense attempted to prove its importance by putting on the best possible show to solidify its role as the dominant ruler. The sense of sight was dressed in impressively colorful clothes, trying to outdo the others. The sense of sound came forward and performed with beautiful enchanting sounds of bells infused with natural beauty. One by one, each of the senses presented its powerful functions, demonstrating its beauty and glory. Each one attempted to outshine the others. Finally, *Prana* stepped forward. The *Prana*, who was so modestly dressed and so unimpressive, got tired of the arrogance of all the senses and announced *Prana* is the most vital, nourishing, and animating of all the senses. Everyone became deeply silent. Suddenly, all of the senses broke out into arguments, each trying to prove its dominance and power over the others. Having heard enough, *Prana* abruptly left the meeting. *Prana* stepped out the door and, within seconds, all other senses started getting weak and fuzzy. Their beauty and glory began to fade, and, suddenly, all the senses begged for *Prana* to return.

Once you recognize that *Prana* is a direct link to the superconscious divine power, you can use it as a powerful tool to dismantle the preprogrammed, conditioned, time-bound past that acts as a blockage in the body, preventing you from accessing this infinite power of the source within. *Prana* opens all the doors for restoring the balance of the body and initiates all healing functions at the very core of your being.

Expectations and interpretations on the level of the ego-mind pass through the body in the form of feelings. Feelings are what you think you are. Anxiety, depression, fear, insomnia, fatigue, and health-related problems that appear in physical form are caused by abusive use of sensory stimulation. When you use addiction as a compensation for stress, you overindulge in food, sex, work, alcohol, and drugs. You reinforce the same symptoms that you are desperately trying to get rid of, and you go against the *Pranic* wisdom of the body. Once you understand the role of *Prana* and how it feeds both unconscious addictive behavior and habit patterns, you can go to the superconscious state of being to liberate the *Pranic* energy trapped in unconscious patterns. Instead of fighting with the symptoms on the surface (in the form of self-destructive habits), you learn how to dismantle the preprogrammed karmic body, removing the cause and releasing the bondage of the past from the karmic body of impressions.

Your Shadow Self and the Button Pusher

The unconscious is popularly recognized as the shadow self, self-image, or karma body. This unconscious center is created by "I am," the soul within you, when identified with your reactive perceptions of reality. When "I am" identifies with reactive thought forms, the "I am" that is formless is turned into the thought forms that you identify with. The reactive thought patterns to which you give a voice are entered as data into the unconscious body. Every personal reaction to reality remains as unresolved experiences of the past, which are incomplete gestalt that gets registered in the unconscious. This incomplete gestalt holds the sub-conscious energy captive in the pattern created by the meaning you gave to that experience that lives in the unconscious karma body. It's like a digital recording. Every time someone pushes the button, the recording plays over and over, as the association with the unre-solved past trauma or hurt is triggered. It resurfaces again and again as a reaction. This kind of reaction is not a punishment but an opportunity. It is a "therapeu-tic irritation," serving as an option to dismantle this unconscious pattern by removing the button rather than the button pusher.

This unconscious body of karma is conditioned by reactive perceptions that are collected in the body of the shadow self-image. These become part of reactive perceptions through which you interact with all the challenges you face in your work life, personal life, and love life. They become your reactions to reality, which is "I am" within you. Every reactive perception and reaction registered in the unconscious karma body lives in perpetual stress-producing conflict within.

A Key Concept: "Energy Follows Attention"

Whenever you seek solutions through the medium of the ego-mind, you move from the source, from the center within, looking at the external world of objects. You want to arrange, manage, and control external relationships, situations, and life conditions. When your attention is shifted to seek love, recognition, approval, or acceptance from others—through the so-called different roles you play, as a lover or beloved, or father or mother, as children, as employer or employee—attention goes into managing external affairs and external relationships. These are the objects.

All such external activities, driven by the ego-mind, appear to be so normal and can be used effectively for success, prosperity, fame, and recognition. But if your attention is excessively engaged in the external world and driven by preprogrammed unconscious patterns, then every interaction with the external world creates internal physical, mental, and emotional conflicts and stress. These are reflected in everything you do, everywhere you go, and every relationship you have.

When attention is engaged in dealing with conflict-creating interactions in the everyday challenges of life, you excessively use up large amounts of *Pranic* energy. The core yogic principle is that "energy follows attention." Each time attention is engaged in stress-producing conflicts with life situations or people, you draw upon the same life-force energy that animates and nurtures health and well-being. You're siphoning energy away from the body's self-regulated, self-balancing, self-healing power and using it to feed unconscious patterns that are not serving you.

As you continue to reinforce these unconscious patterns through reactions to life situations, you use up more *Pranic* energy. This cycle of behavior reinforces the strength of the unconscious self-image. The shadow self is regulated and fed by the ego-mind that thrives on the preprogrammed past and the projected hopes, dreams, and solutions of the future. This is the very same pattern that results in chronic stress.

Capacity of Mind and Time

The ego-mind functions in the dimension of time within a circle of influence on a material plane. Once you discover the source of these internal influences, you'll be released from external sources of stress or circles of concern from others outside of you. When you dismantle this hidden source of stress from within, all other situations—which appear to be causes—instantly disappear. When you change, all changes happen simultaneously. It may feel like stumbling blindly into a room in pitch-black darkness and finally turning on a lamp. Suddenly, the light brings awareness and clarity, and you see everything more keenly. You can now navigate through the room with ease.

Energy is tied to attention, and attention is tied to the unconscious. Beyond the attention that is tied to the preprogrammed past is the connection to the awareness of the "I am" within. The same *Pranic* energy that feeds the self-conscious identification with the preprogrammed conditioned past is also fuel for feeding the superconscious Self.

Yogis who reach the highest level of enlightenment are able to access the cosmic intelligence, sometimes called *akashic* records. They understand the connection to a higher dimension, to opening the channels to clear the passages for the higher wisdom to come through.

Wisdom of Prana—Freedom from Self-Caused Suffering

The *Prana* body plays a significant role in unfolding ultimate freedom from all self-caused suffering. In yogic philosophy, the mind is understood as distinct and separate from the autonomic nervous system, through which the physical body functions in the cosmic rhythm of time and space events. The subconscious *Prana* body is regulated by innate intelligence of the polarity of the autonomic nervous system. This is where the sympathetic and parasympathetic nervous systems carry out the homeostatic self-balancing processes. Its innate manifest intelligence is perceived to be the extension of the unmanifest source of the "being," the "I am" within.

When more tensions are created in the sympathetic nervous system than the parasympathetic system can cope with, the result is stress. The self-image, the being that you are, exists in perpetual conflict, potentially creating chronic stress and dominating the sympathetic nervous system beyond the ability of the parasympathetic nervous system to balance. In turn, these neurological and hormonal imbalances create mental and emotional agitations.

A Deeper Understanding: Going Beyond Limitations

You are born with an individual sense of "I am," allowing you to make individual choices that differ from those of others. Anything you think or say is initiated through the mind; your subconscious *Prana* says "Yes sir" and provides the fuel for carrying out your actions. The mind acts as a reaction to what is present. Witness acts as a response to what is present. You are often taught to be the witness, the observer of these reactions, but what is missing in witnessing is that there is no action. Witness means: "I am the witness. I don't choose. I don't act." The missing link is that, when you are the witness, you must disengage from your ego-mind that is in reaction.

When you withdraw from reaction, you have the ability to respond. When mind and body are in perfect harmony, the *Prana* is the leader, and the mind follows with action. However, in many normal human experiences, when the ego-mind is preprogrammed to react to what is present, the mind occupies the front seat, and *Prana* becomes the slave. The I AM teachings provide an understanding of how to convert reaction into response by using witness.

Once you learn to quiet the mind along with the preprogrammed choice, which is in reaction, *Prana* returns to lead, and balance is restored. When you reach this point, your actions arise from the higher intelligence of *Prana*. What you choose is no longer preprogrammed or the victim of habits, prejudices, likes and dislikes, right and wrong, or good and evil. Even though you are now in action, you are not acting. Simply said, what is acting is the intelligence of *Prana*, not the ego-mind. This is the secret. It is not just saying: "Witness is the solution." Instead, you convert reaction into response, into actionless action, and a paradox begins to happen.

In this way, you enter the dimension of polarity and are in harmony with the whole, because your actions are arising from *Pranic* intelligence, known as instinct. By remaining choiceless, you release personal choice to impersonal intelligence and to the natural laws of unity within and without. You connect to your higher Self, to the divine. When you step out of the preprogrammed past, out of the future, you enter the Zero Stress Zone of Now.

The dilemma is an evolutionary level of human conditions. You have a mind, the most mischievous part of your brain that creates all the nuisances in life. You choose the forbidden fruit of personal choices of liking or disliking, of being attracted or repulsed. You continually search for freedom, which is found only in the merging into oneness within, returning to the source, to the Garden of Eden.

Taking One Step

When you understand these basic principles, you can escape the collective body of human suffering.

You can disengage from reacting to the present. One step eliminates 10,000 steps. To fulfill your choices in the external world, you take 10,000 steps. You choose what you like and become focused on getting what you want. But how many times do you get what you like and then begin disliking it? You are attracted to someone's laughter but, after a while, that very trait becomes an irritant. You finally get that bigger house, but it often becomes just a bigger burden to manage. No one gets divorced who didn't get married. Aversion and addiction come together.

The ego drives one to act in the external world for survival. You enter into an object-bound consciousness of trying to get fulfillment from something outside of yourself. You seek a loving relationship, a new job, or a better car; when you get it, you briefly feel a satisfaction, a sense of happiness. But how long does that feeling of elation last? That is the problem. It is a temporary sense of joy. No matter how much you have—a billion dollars, two airplanes, boats, homes—it is always insufficient. It delivers a false sense of satisfaction, taking you further away from your center. Individuals who boast about possessions—and who are in competition with others to prove they are better—are truly lost.

They have disconnected from their source; most are unaware of how to get back.

How does one return to the source? By learning how to live in response. You can experience it the most when your actions are in direct response to your biological urges. When you're sleepy, you sleep. When you're hungry, you eat. When you're thirsty, you drink.

It might help to visualize the concept as several levels. In the first level, subconscious *Prana* is the ruling energy field that feeds the physical senses. The mental body rules *Prana*. The final level is choiceless awareness, the "I am" that exists beyond the logical, linear, rational dimension of the ego-mind. But since *Prana* is the link between the subconscious and the direct extension of the superconscious state of being, they are both eternal and omnipresent. They are inseparably one. When the "I am" identifies with the time-bound body, it comes in conflict with the timeless being of "I am" and results in perpetual conflict within. The practice of the I AM techniques, such as the Quantum Breath Meditation in Chapter 7, is designed to return back to the *swasthya,* discovering the ultimate source of freedom from all self-caused suffering that gets built into the physical, mental, and emotional bodies.

The subconscious *Prana* body is dominated by your self-conscious ego-mind. Your ego provides the facility for willful action and dominates the subconscious, the innate cosmic intelligence working through your body. This is where personal choice "for or against" the omnipresent presence of this innate intelligence induces the conflict. This is where personal likes and dislikes separate the harmonious interplay of the natural built-in polarity that maintains one's well-being.

In your body, the autonomic nervous system operates through the polarity of the sympathetic and parasympathetic nervous systems. The universal cosmic intelligence maintains the natural circadian rhythms of the breath in and breath out. It maintains the polarities of birth and death, day and night, yin and yang, expansion and contraction, tension and relaxation. All of these represent the innate intelligence of omnipresent, cosmic polarity, where opposites are functioning in harmonious co-creative interplay.

If you excessively activate the left brain through stress-producing, conflict-creating mental and emotional activities, you create more tension through your sympathetic adrenal nervous system than your parasympathetic nervous system can balance. The unresolved tensions result in stress.

Only humans have this self-conscious facility. Animals do not have individual choice to go against the natural circadian rhythms. They are sustained by the simple subconscious autonomic nervous system. They do not develop paranoia, psychosis, or bipolar disease, because they have no freedom to go against universal laws.

The moment self-conscious human beings are born with a facility to go against the universal laws, they are also born with a potential to go beyond them. They can go beyond the confinement of their *Prana* body that manifests through the polarity and return back to the unity that is the source of oneness. This is where you enter into the transcendence of all limitations. You can go beyond the duality of the ego-mind and the polarity of the *Prana* body to enter *Nirvikalpa Samadhi*. This Sanskrit term means "without thought or doubt or mental modification." It is a state beyond understanding, in which the knower and the known are identical, merging into oneness. It is a rare state to achieve; those who have reached it experience a paradigm shift filled with polarities in harmonious interplay. In yogic scriptures, this state is represented by the Third Eye, the 6th Chakra.

Most people live in duality where the perceiver (the subject) remains in perpetual conflict with the perceived (the object). How can you change this?

Chapter 3

The Power of Being

The past and the future are creations of the un-conscious self-image. The present is where the Self is revealed. The secret to uncovering balance in the body is to move from doing to feeling to being, from the future or past to the present, from the time-bound state of body-mind to the timeless state of soul being. Being rooted in the "now" is essential. It is about being in the present moment and not getting caught up in the "what if" or "what will be" but seeing and accepting the "what is."

Finding the Self in the Present

It is a transition from ego-mind that is always "doing" to embracing a relaxed mind in a simple state of being. It is moving from the stress-bound ego that operates as a victim of time past and entering a more expansive, creative dimension of non-linear, non-mental dimension and wisdom. This is fundamental to allow you to remain free from the preprogrammed karmic body of the past, the self-image, and connect to the power of the presence and the power of the Self.

When you're present with whatever you're feeling, you accept yourself as you are. The door to evolution happens not from where you aren't but from accepting and witnessing where you are. Another name for witness and acceptance is *surrender*. You cannot surrender from where you are not. Witness is always present. Only when you witness can the doer disappear; the non-doing presence enters regardless of what is present inside or outside. This is the quintessential solution for all challenges that you face.

The Self-Conscious Ego-Mind

The self-conscious ego-mind drives the *Prana* body as preprogrammed by the conditioned past. But the subconscious *Prana* body that is dominated by the ego-mind is a direct extension of superconscious *Prana*, which is the "I am" within. When "I am"—the son of God, the individual soul within—identifies itself with the preprogrammed body of self-image, the "I am" that is eternal and timeless gets trapped in the dimension of time and acts as the ego-mind.

When you operate through "I am," you do not identify with the preprogrammed, unconscious body. Within each person, "I am" choiceless awareness is the only subject. All other things that come from the external world and manifest from within—in the form of thoughts, feelings, emotions, opinions, self-concepts—are objects. Understanding this energetic anatomy—and how this energy is connected to the unconscious and subconscious *Prana* bodies, self-conscious ego-mind, and superconscious state of being—becomes the link to change and reshape your life.

The Seeds of the Past

Much of your preprogramming comes from the seeds planted in early years by parents, relatives, teachers, and friends. The preprogramming continues into adulthood with more friends and with relationships and spouses. The self-image has been crafted by others and is not who you really are. When you truly "see" yourself, when you remain in choiceless awareness, your spirit will soar, and body, mind, and heart will integrate with spirit.

Knowing Who You Are

Knowing yourself is not the same as knowing about yourself. Whatever you know about yourself is filtered by society and culture. Your entire past, your age, your profession, acquired conditioned thoughts, feelings, self-image and karma body (with all its content) are not you. Think for a moment: if you didn't have your job, your house, and/or your spouse, are you still here? Are you still you? If you had your leg amputated or have a disease, are you still you? Of course. You are the container, the "I am." You are the changeless, timeless soul that was present before you were born into the body you currently inhabit and will continue to be present after your physical body dies. Regardless of what is happening within you or outside of you, you are the "knower." You are the "I am" that is the immortal, timeless, formless being—the container, the consciousness.

The unconditioned "I am" is the container for consciousness. The objects of knowing are the contents that you know about. But when "I am" identifies with reactions such as guilt, blame, shame, hatred, anger, jealousy, fear, and addiction to everything from alcohol to food, work, or sex, the "I am" container turns into a colander. No matter how much content (in the form of achievements of power, property, and skill) you put into this leaky container, the ego-mind remains empty, hungry, and greedy for more. The ego-mind struggles to fill up the container with possessions so it may feel full. But being a leaky container, your ego-mind lives with an insatiable hunger that cannot be satisfied. The appetite of the ego is not real hunger but an illusion. What disturbs you the most is when you believe whatever your mind tells you about yourself. What punches huge holes in the container are beliefs like "I'm not good enough," "I'm too fat," "I'm not worthy of love," and "I don't deserve to be happy." Suffering and discontent begin when you ignore who you really are. What you believe about yourself is not who you are. Confused?

You are full and complete as you are. You may not yet be seeing it. This doesn't mean you don't need the outside for sustenance, survival, health, and well-being of the body. But to get what you need from the outside, you need to be connected on the inside to the source of infinite wisdom and transformative energy.

All the problems you perceive are seen through your reaction as though they are coming from others or from outside of yourself. Therefore, everything you do to solve the problems happens externally. But you have not let go of the internal reaction that was present before the appearance of the outside issue. Efforts to solve problems—by changing external situations without letting go of your reactive perception—change nothing but the content. When you respond to situations with comments such as "He made me so angry" or "She always upsets me," you are blaming others or outside situations for how you feel. How you feel is shaped by reactions and how you are thinking about your feelings.

Thoughts, Feelings, and Emotions Are Not Reality

A woman drives down a highway and sees, in the distance, a dog lying motionless in the road, apparently crushed to death. She is suddenly overwhelmed with a pervasive reaction of sadness and loss for the poor dog, which was obviously hit and killed by a car. She dwells on this profoundly upsetting feeling. Tears well up in her eyes. "The poor, helpless dog," she cries out to herself, as she reflects on the loss of her own dog a few years earlier. She gets more and more upset. She feels a lump in her throat, her heart aches, her stomach becomes nauseated, and her hands get clammy. But as she approaches closer to the stilled brown shape, she sees that it is merely a furled brown towel that had fallen from a car and landed on the road. It is not a dog at all. All the emotions that flooded her body, causing tears and body aches, were not the reality of the moment but, in fact, were created in her own mind—by her own reactions. It was her illusion of reality; yet, it manifested physically in her body.

You do this all the time. You react to situations and to the comments or actions of friends, coworkers, or lovers because of preconceived notions and preconditioned reactions. In this way, you create conflict or miscommunications for yourself. You keep playing the same boring or disturbing recording, with the same old story, and you do nothing to change it.

A young boy is bitten by a dog. When he grows up and becomes a husband and father, he refuses to allow his family to have a dog. His family feels he is being unfair, harsh, and cruel to deny them this sweet pleasure of a pet, but they do not know of his youthful trauma. His fear, instilled by a long-ago experience, is filtering a projection into his life today, and no one—not even him—recognizes or understands the reality of it all.

Consider another example. A woman from Boston, teaching a group of adults, was puzzled by a student who was constantly and brutally negative towards her. The student was downright mean and nasty. The teacher did everything she could to win the student over, but nothing worked. One day, the student mentioned to the teacher that she was the spitting image of her sister. Surprised by the comment, the teacher asked, "And how do you feel about your sister?" The woman replied, "I hate her." So the student's actions today created a total negative reaction to a teacher who reminded her of her sister, which had nothing to do with who the teacher happened to be in the here and now. Think of your own experiences and how many times you might have judged someone hastily before realizing you were wrong. Nothing is more disconcerting than that moment during the middle of an argument when you realize you made a mistake.

Reactions in Disguise

Whatever you experience through your reactive perception arises from your identification with un-resolved, incomplete memories of past experiences. Thought forms are born of the karma body, of the self-image you identify with. When you identify with emo-tional reaction, you are reactivating and replaying the unresolved past, the old recording. You're tormenting yourself with the same hurt you originally experienced. In reality, external objects or situations that trigger reactive perceptions, thoughts, feelings, and actions are not the cause of the conflict but only an outward reflection of your reactive, unconscious body of karma. What happened yesterday is gone. It is merely a memory. But when the reaction of yesterday resurfaces today, you energize the lifeless memory, and it becomes real to you today.

Chapter 1 introduced the concept that "energy follows attention." If you focus on negative thoughts, you're feeding that energy and that way of thinking. If you believe what you think, then your life is shaped by the form you give it through your thoughts. To live in the protective, regenerative, creative power of now, the present, is to accept that the reactive return of emotionally charged thoughts is just a phantom memory. They have no power over you unless you believe them to be true and give them energy by your focus. These memories arise from the graveyard of the dead past or draw from dreams of the future. These memories create internal conflict and stress, preventing your attention from living the life as it happens in the present. If you are present with what is present, you enter the infinite source of *Pranic* energy.

To take a quantum leap from resisting to accepting, begin with an integrative intention that puts you in harmony with your time-bound presence and your timeless being. In this place, you are at peace with yourself as you are. That intention automatically creates a shift, no matter what you might face in that moment. When you accept what is known to you as your self-image and self-concepts and you are open, nothing remains for you to fight with to change. You accept the change that is happening and instantly revert back to witness.

The Button Pusher Is a Mirror

When you have a strong emotional reaction to anyone or any situation, you can be certain it is a reflection of what you are unwilling to embrace in yourself. Whenever you embrace what you face in the outer world, you have accepted the separated part of yourself. The outer world is a creation of your perceived perception. The perceiver in conflict perceives conflict everywhere he goes and in everyone around him. All experiences that appear to be coming from the outer world are just a reflection of the conflicts within you that you have not yet resolved.

Your unconscious karma body remains invisible but becomes visible when some external relationship or situation pushes your karmic button. It then resurfaces in you and holds the object or person who pushed your button as responsible for causing you to have a reaction. "He is so arrogant" and "She gets me so frustrated" are typical reactions. When you are blind to the source of suffering, you try to eliminate the button-pusher and save the button. When you are conscious, you see that the button-pusher is not the problem. Your reactive karma button is the problem. Instead of reacting to the button-pusher, you just learn to remove the karmic button. For instance, instead of getting a divorce, you might consider divorcing yourself from the buttons. If you have no buttons to push, there will be no button-pusher. This is called enlightenment. An ancient Vedic proverb says: "The measure of your enlightenment is your level of comfort with your own paradoxes.

Presence Is Undivided

From time immemorial, people have been pondering the question: "Who am I?" Today, that question has perhaps more relevance and urgency than ever before. Our high-tech, high-stress existence is focused on having more, getting more, and becoming more. But does your attempt to find fulfillment outside of yourself result in anything other than ongoing frustration? The irony is that, as you are driven by searching for possessions, power, and prestige, you only find yourself more isolated, lonely, and lacking. These internal conflicts and stresses are reflected in your interactions with loved ones and in your external lives. Your behavior with others may be loaded with your expectations, which are reactions in disguise; once you react to them, you are relating not to the present but to the past that appears to be present. Living in conflict, cut off from others and from the source of life within you, you suffer. You are discontent. You get depressed, turning to distractions, drugs, or alcohol to make you feel better. These are temporary and hazardous solutions.

Your ego-mind is conditioned by social norms and personal likes and dislikes. You have been preconditioned to evaluate and judge each present moment by the understandings that have been conveyed to you by your parents, teachers, friends, spouses, and even your children. The ego lives in perpetual conflict with reality—in duality, in service of the self-image.

In reality, what is present is present. You can't enhance or diminish what is present; you can only acknowledge and embrace it. But the ego-mind fights with the present; it runs from the present or attempts to modify or control it. It's not easy to learn how to accept what is as it is. When you learn that lesson—to accept what is, without judgment—you are liberated to enjoy a more effortless life.

Presence is undivided; choosing for or against is what gives birth to the ego-mind. Choice separates you from the source of Oneness, from the flow of life. Once ego chooses for or against, then you are required to do something. But if you remain the choiceless witness, there remains nothing for you to do. Ego disappears, and you enter the Zero Stress Zone of non-doing presence. You merge into Oneness. How do you achieve this?

Choiceless Awareness Is the Solution to the Real Problem

You can achieve choiceless awareness by shifting from thinking to feeling. Feeling activates the undistorted wisdom of the body in the form of vital life energy, *Prana*. It reveals what is beyond preprogrammed choices of right or wrong and what is present beyond time. In the light of conscious awareness, it reveals the true meaning of what is right or wrong. When you create a shift from the preprogrammed ego-mind to the *Prana* or cosmic intelligence, all actions that arise from that *Prana* manifest as a direct response to that cosmic intelligence. The result is balance and harmony. People continue to suffer and struggle when they rely on the ego to solve the problems of life rather than having the faith to accept what is present and accepting and relaxing with it.

The Integrated Amrit Method (I AM) approach is a paradigm shift from the separative ego-mind to a co-creative partnership with the *Prana* body. It is a transition from the animal instinctive consciousness to the spirit being that you are. The Amrit lineage has discovered that the secret of the Holy Spirit is as universal *Prana*, which animates the entire body of creation and the human body. The "I am," the soul, manifests as spirit *Prana*. In essence, it is your divine potential.

When movements are guided by the direct promptings of *Prana*, you are moving on the pathless path, in action-less, ego-less action. In this state, all questions are resolved through promptings of vital life force energy or *Pranic* presence rather than through the preconditioned ego-mind. That guidance from *Prana* is not prelearned. The biological *Prana* body operates in the subconscious dimension that is self-regulating, homeostatic, self-balancing, and self-healing.

Understanding Polarity and Duality

In the body, you have primal sensations connected to sustenance and survival. Health and well-being of the body operate according to complementary polarity. In polarity, positive and negative are in complementary interplay, such as with breath in and breath out, night and day, hot and cold, tension and relaxation. In polarity, there is balance. There is unity and oneness. One element cannot exist without the other, like birth and death.

When the mind operates in conflict, it creates stress-producing duality and upsets the natural balance. Energy becomes fractured, fragmented. You feel unfocused or overwhelmed. When you are attached to what you like, you have fear of losing it. This engages your attention to maintain control or seek more of what you like. Any addiction to pleasure comes with the fear of losing it or not having enough. This demands a lot of attention. The stronger the addiction, the stronger the fear—and the greater the attention it consumes. The energy that follows this attention gets wasted in self-destructive ways. The body's wisdom becomes dominated by thoughts and emotions; the *Prana* energy serves the whimsy of the ego-mind, pulling the biological *Prana* from its involuntary, self-regulating, balancing processes into conflict in order to support the energy demands of the ego's fight-or-flight response.

In conflicting duality, positive is "for" and negative is "against" something or someone. At that point, energy is disturbed or blocked, and you enter a state of disintegration, which may show up as restlessness, confusion, chaos, anxiety, or depression. You are far from the integrated state of the Zero Stress Zone.

When your practice is goal-oriented, your ego says, "I'll celebrate when I'm successful, when I have that big house or the top job or that perfect spouse." You defer happiness to some time in the future. But life is a celebration from moment to moment. When you accept yourself and go where you are going and do what you are doing by being who you are, the door opens, and you are on your way to deep integration and harmony with the whole that you are.

Anything that you do to become whole by getting what you want is an illusion. You can become whole by being whole at every moment of your journey towards oneness. And to become whole means to accept wherever you are, whatever you are doing, and whomever you are with.

You can be whole only in the present. That means you can be total only where you are, regardless of what conditions prevail within and without. This is called surrender, which allows you to surrender to *Prana*. *Prana* does the rest. Surrender means simply trusting that the higher power will guide you. When you are fearful, you take charge of changing. When you have faith, you let the changeless part of your being do all that is necessary. And how can you begin that journey? With trust in your own higher self. You know everything you need, when you need it, and the process of how to get it. That is called innate intelligence of your body and inborn potential. Your whole body is animated and maintained by that intelligence, which should be enough proof for you to trust it and move from subconscious to superconscious witness.

Chapter 4

The Mysterious Source Within

As mentioned in chapters 1 and 3, energy follows attention. If attention is absorbed in toxic thoughts or situations, energy gets dispersed and dissipated. If attention is inwardly focused, the *Prana* held hostage in the body can be released, freeing this vital energy for accelerated well-being, balance, and harmony.

An Experience in Stillness

Experiment with the following simple exercise. It is best if you can make a quick digital recording of your voice or have someone read this to you very slowly; but if you're unable to do that, just try to remember the steps and notice how energy moves in your body. Sit comfortably in a chair or on the floor.

Begin to vigorously rub your palms together until energy begins to flow through them and you feel heat being generated. Then, gently wipe tensions from your face. Place the palms of your hands flat, so they rest against your face, with your fingertips resting lightly on your eyelids or just above the eyebrows. There should be no space between the palms and face. Inhale and exhale. Let go and relax. Let go of all expectations. Take a breath in and exhale. Let go of all tensions. With the intention of feeling the energy in your hands, wipe away any tightness and fatigue from your face. Using your fingertips, gently massage your forehead, temples, ears, cheeks, and jaws, and around the mouth and neck. Your breath should be uniform and steady. Take a deep breath in and let go. This process creates a transition from external awareness to inward focus.

Keeping your eyes closed, place your hands in your lap and follow these directions for a simple breathing technique. Because breath can bring you into a deeply relaxed space, keep your eyes closed and internalize your attention. Sit tall. Take a breath in and exhale through gently pursed lips, as if you are blowing through a straw. Keep your eyes closed and continue this breathing. As you inhale, breathe in joy and harmony. As you exhale, let your exhalation be long, steady, and unbroken. Blow out all worry, fear, or tension. Repeat this breath seven times. Then breathe naturally. Relax.

Empty your mind and drop into innermost stillness. Allow yourself to feel the energetic sensations as induced by the deep breathing. As you stir up energy in your body, you release tensions. Experience the pulsating energy field in your arms, in your body, in your face. Relax. Allow yourself to drop into the next level of inner stillness. Let go even more. Drop into a deep level of tranquility and peace. Bring your attention to the spot between your eyebrows in the middle of your forehead, known as your Third Eye. Let your mind completely melt and merge into the energy pulsating and flooding your entire body. Next, notice your arms. Bring your attention to your arms, where you can feel much more clearly the pulsating energy field. Let your arms hang by your side; as they hang there, bring your attention to your palms. Attention and energy begin to flood into those palms very clearly. Shift your attention to your right arm and only your right arm. Feel it. Then shift it to the left arm and only the left arm. Notice how the energy pours into your left arm. Next, bring attention to both arms. Once again, bring your attention to the space between your eyebrows and feel your mind completely melt and merge into it. Just become aware of how calm your mind is, how relaxed your body is, how peaceful and soft your breath is. When you are ready, take a deep inhalation and very gradually open your eyes.

When you were directed to feel the energy in your right arm, did your attention follow that energy? Could you feel sensations in your right arm and then your left arm? It may take time to notice these sensations, because you are not yet conditioned to being aware of them. At the very least, you should feel a lot calmer than when you began the exercise.

Shifting From Reactive Thinking

When your body is tensed and in high alert, caught up in reaction, you feel overwhelmed, uneasy, and uncomfortable. You may deal with those unpleasant sensations with outbursts of anger, slumps into depression, or bouts of irritability. Stress turns you into a loser regardless of what game you play, whether it is love, business, or family life. These are all mind games. They're all created on an ego level. When you learn how to release the stress by restoring balance, releasing the tension, you feel better. The Experience in Stillness can help create the shift. You'll notice a new sense of relief. You'll see situations more clearly. You'll see with more clarity, objectivity, and understanding. You'll feel the sense of joy and fulfillment return when you are connected to the flow of *Prana*.

When you are alert and aware, you will be able to catch yourself in the midst of emotional reaction. When you notice your first reaction, you can arrest the reaction to create an extraordinary shift; this dismantles your preprogrammed past and prevents it from being reinforced with a second reaction or a destructive chain of reactive thoughts. By stopping the reactive behavior that arises from the karmic body of the unresolved past impressions, you seize an opportunity to erase unconscious connections. Whenever you react to your first impression, you reinforce your preprogrammed past. The moment you learn how to withdraw from it, you are starving the body of the self-image to death. If you fight with it, you feed it. If you stop it, you kill it and eliminate struggle.

In order to enter the presence that you are, you have to withdraw attention from your first reaction, or *pratyahara*. The first reaction is time-bound action that resurfaces in the form of reaction in the present. Choiceless awareness prevents you from habitually, mechanically, and unconsciously getting caught in the second reaction. The absence of reaction to the first reaction becomes a portal to freedom from your time-bound ego-mind.

Escape From the Prison of the Past to the Freedom of the Present

Whenever you find yourself having an emotional re-action to someone, notice that everything you are voicing through your reaction is preprogrammed by your conditioned past. Once you learn to withdraw reactive thoughts, you shift from your thinking center and bring it into your energy body, to your feeling center, such as with the Experience in Stillness technique.

When reactive thoughts flood your mind, your entire body begins to react: you get sweaty, or your heart begins to race. When caught in emotional reactions, you lose all sense of objectivity and clarity. You lose touch with your feeling center. Anything you do that is reactive has always proved to be self-destructive and creates more problems than it solves. As a result, if you choose to withdraw from this reactive pattern, if you pause and take a few deep breaths, you create the shift from the thinking center to the feeling center, where the emotionally charged frequency of the energy field in your body is brought into harmony and balance.

In Chapter 7, you will read about how to do the full Quantum Breath Meditation technique.

Restoring Balance

The moment you shift from reactive thinking to witnessing the energy field that is processing the emotional reaction, you may feel discomfort as your *Pranic* body restores balance. Allow yourself to settle without returning to the reactive thoughts. Trust. Just as water seeks its own surface, your energy body restores its own harmony. When you withdraw your mind and detach from your thinking center, the body balances with its own innate intelligence, and the impact of the emotional agitations on the energy body is removed.

As you transfer into non-reactive perception, you will see the other side with objectivity and will transcend from non-communicative reactive mode into creative communication mode. In this way, you restore the ability to solve the problem that you previously faced with emotionally-charged reactions. This clarity appears in your physical posture, countenance, eyes, and verbal expressions, as you become calmer and more at peace. You move from your rationalizing left brain into the creative reasoning that allows you to see yourself and the other person or situation more clearly and in the light of compassion. When you are emotional, your body's vibrations are dissonant and out of balance. The moment you relax into what is present, you change the chemistry of your body. Once you create the shift from the reactive mode of being into non-reactive receptive mode, you create a hormonal change that will diffuse the stressful moment. The process works for 9-year-olds as well as for 90-year-olds!

From Darkness to Light

The key is to shift from reactive choice to choiceless awareness. This creates a transition from the preprogrammed shadow self-image of the past, as it is exposed to the light of choiceless awareness. There is no struggle between darkness and light. The light of choiceless awareness automatically and effortlessly dismantles the reactive emotional patterns without ever requiring a fight-or-flight reaction.

It is the combination of thought forms and energy that creates a physical experience and translates this into chemical, physical, or biological changes in the body. When you change your reactive thought forms into formless states of non-reaction, you are exposing the darkness of your preprogrammed conditioned past to the omnipresent presence of the light of consciousness. Every time you shift from reactive perception to non-reactive choiceless awareness, you dismantle the unconscious patterns held in the shadows of your self-image. You release these from the unconscious karma body, stored in the form of psychosomatic blocks. The trapped energy of the unconscious is released into light of consciousness.

Every reaction arises out of the split for or against; the entire body of the preprogrammed past is built like this. The moment you choose for or against what is present—the moment you judge someone or some situation--the presence in you that is formless descends into the reactive choice and enters the form, becoming time-bound. The results are statements like "I am upset," "I am unhappy," and "He makes me tense." As Plato once said, beauty is in the eye of the beholder. The same is true of distorted reactive perception; that, too, is in the eye of the beholder. The moment you are caught in your reaction, everything that you see about the other is a reflection of you.

This means that everything you see about external situations or conditions or the people you face is a mirror image that reveals what is invisible in you. Thus, the world acts like a biofeedback machine. Every reaction that emerges out of your past is not a punishment but an opportunity for you to convert the blocked shadow energy and transform it into the light of consciousness.

The reality is that presence consists of form that is present in manifest reality and formless in unmanifest reality. The ancient yogic scriptures say: "*Pinde so Brahmande*," which means "what is in the macrocosm is in the microcosm." What is without is within. Your center is the timeless container.

The Posture of Consciousness

Within each person exist thoughts and thought-lessness, form and formless presence, sound and silence, action and actionless stillness. External reality consists of forms and formless space. Space is eternal, omnipresent, unmanifest, formless presence. All the multitudes of forms in space—galaxies, stars, moons, and planets—are all changing forms. Your body, senses, feelings, and thoughts are changing forms contained within the formless silence and stillness of the space within. Eckhart Tolle refers to it as the "Power of Now."

In the practice of the Posture of Consciousness, deliberate action moves you towards the non-doing integrative state of being. You drop into non-doing presence. In that state of content-less consciousness, you connect with your Self. You know and accept who you are. You recognize the authentic you—the being who is divine creation without the layers of judgment or criticisms heaped on from a past perspective of teachers, parents, or friends. You discover the real you, the child within who is full of purity and joy. When you empty your mind of reactive thoughts and feelings about yourself, what remains is the essence of your being. You are non-reactive presence. You merge into Oneness in the Zero Stress Zone. It is a place of blissful happiness, and yet, you are still aware of external issues or challenges that you may need to address. You will find that you can handle these situations from a more integrated effective place, and the solutions are far more obvious.

All Answers Are Consciousness

In the 1970s, Patricia Stevens was a young mom with three children, the youngest of whom was autistic. Few people understood or knew how to treat or manage autism in those years. As she describes it, she was "in overload." Then, she heard a brief lecture by Yogi Amrit Desai at the dedication of a yoga studio in Indianapolis. The message she heard most loudly from Gurudev was: "You had to live in the what is, not the what should be ... giving up all expectations and having no demands." She recounts: "I thought it was the silliest thing I ever heard. Having no expectations basically meant we weren't going to make it ... where I was ... I had to really work hard."

"Six months later I went to an intensive workshop (taught by Gurudev). It was a really wild thing to do first ... it was three days of sitting cross legged and answering one question: 'Who are you?' From 4 a.m. to 10 p.m. every day. Just blew everything wide open. When I got home, my sister just looked at me and said 'What's happened to you? You're glowing.' Then, people started making comments about how I changed, looked different. I felt different ... calmer. That sold me." Through the wisdom of Yogi Amrit Desai, she found the strength to break through medical boundaries and find answers to raising her son. She even authored a book, *Small Pastures,* which eloquently recounts her courageous experiences and details how her connection to Gurudev helped her through such a painful journey.

Today, decades later, Stevens splits her time between Colorado and Ocala, Florida, and is still committed to the teachings. As a rolfer, Stevens incorporates the teachings in her work. She notes: "To really do a good job, you have to be the rolfer. You leave your story and your needs behind, and you're there. We learned by watching Gurudev consistently through the years. He could leave a meeting that was, to other people, overwhelming and upsetting—and within 10 minutes after leaving that meeting, he was seated on a chair bringing everyone into deep meditation. He could just shift. That's what I want to learn how to do. I watch it and I'm getting better and better at it. It really helps working with kids—even adult kids. You see something going on, and you have a mother's response, reactive, and you know that's not going to be helpful. I can now stay in the detached yogic place and stay in the moment, instead of getting into the story and how I want to make someone different and make my life better as a mother."

Stevens' most profound and overwhelming insight from the teachings is that "all answers are in consciousness and come from within you." She comments: "As soon as you know you're not conscious and you're in a story, you're ineffective. You've got to get back to consciousness." How does one accomplish that? Stevens offers: "We've used the 'breathe, relax, and let go' everywhere and in every aspect of our lives with every moment—and with our clients. Unless you're in that consciousness, you're just running a tape, and you're a victim of stress. If you can get really quiet by yourself, then you hear it and experience it. I have learned consciousness is the answer. It holds every answer, if you can just get conscious. But you have to stop and breathe to get that answer."

Her sincerest advice is: "Do what brings you peace. And spiritually, doing anything that removes the obstacles ... it's about creating a lifestyle that's peaceful. If you disturb others, your peace will be disturbed. If you are violent to someone, you are, in reality, violent to yourself. Sometimes, making that decision for peace is against what one might want to do. It's hard. People don't understand that your commitment to a good breakfast can change your whole day, and it's hard to do. So you have to find what works for you and find the courage to do it," she asserts.

Raising her adopted autistic son, Stevens overcame all odds, and today her son is doing brilliantly. She states that, in order to do what her son needed, "I had to really get detached and be so completely accepting of where he was and how he was. I had two biological kids. I understood them and could feel what they needed. But this kid (with autism) was out there. I had to get so conscious and stay so detached that I could connect to where he was. He was my gift, because then I stopped expecting so much from the other kids."

"You can choose being peaceful instead of going back to your crazy mind."

—Patricia Stevens, rolfer and author of *Small Pastures* (Ocala, Florida)

Chapter 5

Discovering Heaven on Earth

Stress has an edge. Whenever a situation drives you to the edge, you have an emotional reaction. The reaction manifests in the form of fight or flight. This edge is your tolerance point, where you get edgy, angry, frustrated, or fearful, and it is triggered whenever you face a challenging situation in any part of your life. Reality is omnipresent; an edge is personal.

Deep Seeds

When you are under stress, you are in conflict with the omnipresent presence that you are. This conflict between you and your Self is what is revealed. What had remained invisible becomes visible, as an edge, when some external situation triggers your edginess.

This happens frequently in relationships, where deep seeds about your Self are revealed. For instance, a couple is getting ready to go out to dinner. The husband comments that he likes his wife's hairstyle, the way she's put it up off her shoulders. But rather than hearing the reality of what he is saying, the wife hears, "He doesn't like my hair when it is down. He won't love me anymore if I wear my hair down." The deep seed that is surfacing is one that addresses her own perceptions about self-worth and self-image—that she won't measure up to his expectations if she doesn't wear her hair in a certain way. And she may fear a loss of his love. While this may sound extreme, these seeds are at the very core of relationships, and most are planted around the most profound human need: to be loved.

As your stress level goes up, you become the carrier of stress, which represents your inner conflict. In the previous example of the wife, her insecurities may also become expressed in poor interactions with her boss or even her parents, because her deeply planted seed about self-worth will be carried into each relationship—until she addresses it.

When You Change Your Self, the Whole World Changes With You

When you are under stress, your thoughts, emotions, and internal conflicts go everywhere you go—into every relationship, every place, every situation. Even when you plan a vacation, as a way of releasing stress and leaving conflict at home to "get away from it all," you still carry the "I am" that you are with you wrapped up in thoughts, emotions, and reactions. So wherever you go, there you are. That is why the practice of Zero Stress Zone is not about trying to release the stress by trying to manage or manipulate external situations, conditions, and relationships. Rather, when you change your self, the whole world changes with you.

You cannot live in the same self-destructive habit patterns in stress-producing conflict and hope to have a different life. The Zero Stress Zone changes stress from its very core rather than changing the external conditions that trigger it. Once you identify with your restless, agitated mental and emotional conditions, no matter what conditions you change externally, you remain the victim of the internal conflicts. The real solution is accessing the Zero Stress Zone, where happy hormones like serotonin and melatonin are released, reducing pain and emotional reactions automatically without side effects.

A Metaphor for Life

The skills of mindful attention and meditative aware-ness create a calm mental attitude that can be developed by practicing silent moments to drop into the deepest levels of your Self. The impact of this deep relaxation technique extends to all challenges you encounter in life. The benefits are cumulative and profound.

Often, when you are doing yoga or playing a sport, the ego-mind becomes the performer, and the mind is actively engaged in self-criticism, comparing your performance and judging yourself against others. Your mind is agitated and engaged in internal conflict, even as your body is engaged in performing. As a result of constant internal conflict, your mind is restless. Whenever you are mentally agitated and emotionally reactive to whatever you are facing at any given moment, you are engaged by external motivation in the posture of ego. You are giving away your energy and entering a state of disintegration.

Imagine a light shining on a painting. If the light has a red filter, then the colors of the painting will interact with the red light to appear differently; white will appear pink or red, yellow will appear orange, green will appear black. If the light has no filter, the painting will appear in its true colors. In the same way, when you view a life situation through the personalized, reactive perspective of your conditioned past, people and events may appear to be adverse or in your favor. When you can remove the filter of your habitual way of thinking and seeing, you gain access to neutral reality. You see the situation as it is, devoid of personal interpretation. This is the true reality.

The Controlling Ego-Mind Affects Quality of Life

External conditions are transitory. Working hard to change external situations is not a solution. When faced with the challenges of life, people who are caught in ordinary consciousness struggle to change other people, external conditions, or life situations by increasing their creativity, efficiency, information, and technical skills. Even if they appear to solve the problem in the beginning, every solution turns into another problem in the end.

Lasting joy, success, and fulfillment in life come from the internal work of removing reactive tendencies. Many times, external conditions in life need to be modified and improved. You must have the ability to manage external affairs. But external conditions, no matter how well they are organized for your comfort, pleasure, and fulfillment, cannot solve the stress-creating reactions and conflicts that you create moment to moment in situations that you face. If you haven't worked internally to release the habits of the control-ling ego-mind that keep you trapped in reaction, nothing that you achieve or possess will ever make a difference in your quality of life.

Actions based on distorted perception may initiate changes in an external situation, but they are never effective in solving a problem. When you react to reaction, you are attempting to solve the problem of the past in the future, where it can never be solved on an internal or an external level. All problems that appear to be coming from outside yourself are truly the prob-lems of reaction. You react to what you perceive to be coming from the other person or the situation. Trying to solve a problem in time by planning a solution in the future, you change external situations and condi-tions—the contents of consciousness—but you haven't changed the consciousness that was distorted by your reaction. Remember the reaction to the dog that ap-peared to be lying crushed on the highway? It was a totally distorted reaction.

Whole-Brain Thinking

A knee-jerk reaction is automatic and unconscious. It arises out of your past and can be dismantled only in the present. Unconscious reactions happen automatically, but there is a part of you that is conscious and can witness and change your reaction. When you change your reaction, you change from the core. You change intensely. You shift your consciousness to accept the truth of what is instead of reacting to external conditions. This is your divine potential. Accessing your divine potential has nothing to do with what you are doing but rather with how you are doing what you are doing.

Reactive thinking is fear-based and characterized by the projection of awareness into the past or future. Fear is what takes you into the external situation in the wrong way and shows you a problem where the problem is not. Whenever you are caught in an internal reaction, your sensitivity is gone. You are completely out of touch with your body, and your nervous system is processing the friction.

The shift from problem solving to creative expression happens in the integrated state of being when awareness is grounded in the direct experience of the present moment. When you feel sweetness in your body and hear "Aha!" in the mind, you have entered the alpha state, where healing occurs spontaneously. You are connected to your *Prana* body—your own internal sense of being alive. You relax and enjoy life, and your creativity naturally increases. Neither money nor convenience can give you this experience. When you move into alpha-theta brain waves, scientists call it "whole-brain thinking."

This is an internal condition you create that connects you with the joy of life and naturally brings fulfillment. The *Prana* energy body gives you the connection to the soul. When your perception comes from the soul, it comes with great ecstasy. You cannot get that from outside or from people telling you that you are great. Rather, external fulfillment will come as a result of your primary commitment to connecting to the source within. Then, you not only become prosperous, but you are able to maintain your quality of life. The rare combination of prosperity and happiness will begin. This is the shift from problem solving to creative expression in life.

Harness the Indestructible Power of the Presence

Choiceless awareness is like a fire burning the rope that binds you to the self-destructive body of your masked self-image. It is a non-linear process. If you take a rope and wrap it around a post a hundred times clockwise, the linear solution is to unravel the rope by unwrapping it a hundred times counterclockwise. True presence is a quantum leap beyond the traditional psychology of working it out through your mind.

Albert Einstein observed: "You cannot solve a problem with the same mind that created the problem." The Integrative Amrit Method (I AM) is designed to go beyond the rational mind and dismantle the reactive karmic pattern through the light of consciousness that does not fight with the reaction. It simply brings the light of consciousness that effortlessly burns the old karma. Every reactive experience that is built into the body of karma came out of choice for or against what is present. Every choice that a person has is built around the preprogrammed past—that when you are for what is present you call it "good," and when you are against, you call it evil. This is clearly represented in the story of Adam and Eve. Once you choose the fruit of knowledge that divides the whole into good and evil, you are thrown out of the Garden of Eden. This separation of good and evil creates separation from the source, a disconnection from the presence within. That separated self-image, also called the prodigal son, is ejected from the Garden of Eden and becomes the victim of all the self-caused suffering. You call it hell. It is full of pain.

How do you find your way back to the Garden of
Eden? The portal back to heaven on earth is the reverse
of choice. It is choiceless, non-reactive awareness to
what is present externally. By practicing non-reaction to whatever you face from moment to moment
in the external world, you bring the self-image into
harmony, into reconnecting with your omnipresent
presence. It brings the prodigal son back to the father.
Choiceless awareness becomes the opening to return
to the Garden of Eden, to come back in tune with what
God wanted for you at the beginning. This choiceless
awareness is the same as what Christ said: "Thy will
be done, not Mine." When you shift from choice to
witness, you are returning back to the Garden of Eden,
as God wanted for Adam and Eve. It is a return to the
innocence and purity that renounces personal choice
for or against what is present and lives in response to
God's will.

The Omnipresent Timeless State of Being

So what is God's will? When you enter into
choiceless awareness, you disengage from the preprogrammed past and enter the omnipresent presence,
the "I am." You enter into the power of God within and
experience the "I am that I am." All I AM techniques

are designed to help you disengage from the time-bound body of karma and enter into the timeless state of being that you are.

Inner Sanctuary

"I had started a 12-step program to avoid my desire to go through life in an unconscious state, because it had gotten so painful. I couldn't turn off the tape that constantly played in my head. These teachings transformed me. I am thrilled to have learned that my ego has been at the core of my problems and that I just need to shut the door on it. I can be in my inner sanctuary in just minutes ... my own blessed Zero Stress Zone."

—S. Brick, gallery owner, Naples, Florida

Chapter 6

Embracing Change Without Reaction

The path to integration and feeling good is letting go of ego. To accomplish this, witness your thoughts without engaging in them. By allowing them to just drift through your awareness, you shift your consciousness. The preceding thought has already collapsed and vanished. The succeeding thought has not yet been created. In the gap between the two is the field of infinite possibilities. In this domain of silence, you enter a non-ego state of being: a divine place where you are not trying to control, manage, or change. It is where you, the doer, become absent in the gap, and the non-doing presence that you are emerges. When you identify with your reactive thoughts, you are in your ego—your phantom, shadow, or manmade self. When you step aside and give yourself permission to drop into relaxation and stillness, you open the opportunity to connect with your authentic self, the integrated oneness that you are.

Reaction Separates You From the Source

All reaction occurs as a coping mechanism. It extends unresolved fears of the past into the present. And who is the carrier? Ego. It is a defense against current possibilities or a fear of the unknown future. Your self-image reacting to an event is a denial of the opening that reality provides.

A New Opening in Silence

All possibilities are open, and you can return to Self as Source when you are daring enough to leap into the present without a reaction, without resistance to what is happening now. So trust not in defensive reasoning but in the reason that helps you bear reality with joy. In the absence of a reactive defense, surrender the self-image. When you do, you appear differently to everyone present. There is a new kind of opening that happens in your being when you enter the state of non-reaction. This place of silence is the gap where you are simply witnessing passing thoughts and feelings without identifying with them. You are the observer, just watching everything that comes within the field of awareness, as though you were watching images flickering across a television screen. They are just colors and images, floating by without emotional content—just light and texture, without interpretations, without emotions.

The absence of reaction is a place of deep relaxation. It is in a non-mental place, a feeling that is integrated into oneness of being. It is the active expression of love—a divine love that is not sheltered and shadowed by the ego or self-concepts. Love itself will teach you, once you learn how to enter the place of quiet meditation. Whether or not you practice will be up to you and to your willingness to rise above your ego.

Meditation is a technique for creating opportunity for silence and, in time, can create a greater gap. Often, people have a belief that they simply are incapable of meditating. If that was your immediate reaction, you are allowing your ego-mind to control you. There are many ways to dismantle the power of the ego-mind and be able to reach a place of deep stillness. Let go and trust that you can learn to meditate. You can access the source within. It is not complicated. It merely takes a first step, a commitment from you. It encourages your own experimentation, an openness, and a desire to improve your life.

More About Self-Image Defense

Your self-image is made up of your conditioned belief system. It operates like a programmed computer, directing your perceptions and activities. The self-image guides your actions within and creates conflict with everyone you encounter. It's a major source of stress. These inner conflicts manifest as self-criticism, anger, fear, blame, or shame. If attention is emotionally charged in reactive behaviors, you're depleting life energy by investing in self-destructive modes. Your actions use up the real life force of *Prana* and choke life out of real potential. If you identify with your self-image whenever it is challenged, *you* feel challenged. This identification with it is what turns your experience into self-destructive perception of reality.

Resistance is rationalized and greatly justified. But that reaction is just a fight against that which is disturbing to your self-image. If you feel frustrated or abused, you compensate by reactive actions and maneuvers to defend your hurt. It becomes defensive reinforcement of your self-concept, further separating you from the higher self that you are. When you are separated from the source in this way, whatever you do comes from the ego-mind. Even performing "good," socially acceptable acts fails to connect you to the true

Self, and you will merely fall prey to your conditioned belief system.

Awakening Out of the Dreams of Self-Concepts

The absence of reaction happens only if you trust that the gap generated by letting go of resistance creates the possibility for awakening out of the dream of self-concepts. When you do not react to defend yourself, your false identity with self-image is put aside. You cease to protect the image. The gap of meditative, choiceless awareness is created. In that gap is the surrender of self-image and the resurrection of the Self. It is a silent invocation of the presence of a divine entity—a spirit guide—to provide the deepest possible shift for yourself and for everyone around you.

The Spiritual Journey

What is good for your soul is a threat to your self-image, your ego. When you embark upon the spiritual journey, you resist what looks negative and chase desired positive or spiritual results. This may look like a normal thing to do, but it is the deceptive work of the ego. It is reaction that reinforces your self-image. When you take the position of being for or against, you are in reaction to what is present rather than acknowledging and accepting what is present.

When you remain in choiceless witness with what you are facing externally, you remain an undivided presence. When you react to what is present outside, you are reinforcing the separation from the presence that you are. In other words, you are reacting to the omnipresent presence with your conditioned preprogrammed past, which causes anxiety and stress. And you truly create your own reality.

Whatever you are facing at any given moment in your life, when you are able to stop being for positive and against negative, you enter the silence. The gap is created. It is in this absence of reaction that there is witness. Silent observation is the most spiritual way of being in the presence of both positive and negative experiences. Witness embraces both positive and negative experiences, without choice for or against. Witness unconditionally accepts what is as is.

You Literally Eat Your Own Emotions

When you shine light on negativity, it disappears. If thoughts, actions, and feelings arise out of your preprogrammed shadow self, they cannot be digested by the body. Unmetabolized experiences cause blocks of insensitivity that become unconsciousness. All undigested experiences have a toxic effect on both body and mind, as they block the flow of energy. Reactions reinforce toxicity.

The Truth About Happiness

If you create external conditions, situations, and relationships for your happiness, they are undependable. Regardless of what you change, everything in the external world continues to change, whether you like it or not. Anything you change as a compensation for your unhappiness will result in your perpetual feeling of fear. Every solution that you are seeking in the world of change creates a sense of insecurity and anxiety. This occurs not only while you are changing it but also afterward. Many people depend on change for their happiness but, at the same time, are afraid of making a change. After having changed what they wanted, they change their liking for what they have changed and are no longer happy with the change. The dimension of change as a solution to happiness remains elusive. As soon as you get there, you're not happy with where you are. It's like flying faster to find the horizon where sky meets the earth. It's unattainable. What appears to be a solution in the future is itself a problem that cannot be solved, no matter what you change in the future. Therefore, what you really seek is the changeless being that you are.

When you are unhappy, the whole world is unhappy with you—but what you are seeing outside is not the reality of what is outside. You are seeing through the masks of your mind, the disturbances that you are to yourself. For example, you may believe that if your spouse is happy with you, you'll be happy with your spouse, and you may expect your spouse to behave in such a way so that nothing disturbs you. It's a nice philosophy, but it is a pursuit of an illusion that doesn't exist. What is the illusion? What you're trying to get from your spouse isn't available. It can be found only within you by restoring your connection to the integrative self of being that you are.

Many people are motivated to achieve more, own more property, or have more nice things, but they're stressed throughout the path towards so-called self-fulfillment. They believe that they can relax and be happy when they retire. Yet all along the way, they practice conflicts and stress in order to be happy; throughout their journey of life, they're miserable. How does that work? It doesn't. If you are doing something for happiness, be happy all along the way.

What Happens When You Marry Your Expectations

You may believe that, if you can rearrange, modify, improve, control, and manage external situations—such as your marriage, working situation, housing, or possessions—you'll be happy. Strangely enough, most people believe this to be true. Of course, there is a necessity to manage external affairs as far as your personal survival is concerned. You need to attend to the sustenance of your health and the well-being of your body. When you care for your body, which is an external phenomena, remember that it is in service of the internal being that you are. Thus, if you make the external affairs you must manage the highest priority, and all of your attention is engaged in solving external problems—such as making sure your children or spouse behave the way you expect—you will enter the land of illusion. Why did you think life could be managed like that? It's that belief system that reveals why it is so dangerous to get married to your concepts. Your marriage does not fail; your expectations do. Any time you marry any kind of situation—whether it is a work situation, a vacation, or a picnic, for example—on the basis of expecting what you will get out of it, you disconnect with reality. *Expectations are frustrations waiting to happen.* By letting go of expectations, you enter the dimension that Buddhists call "beginner's mind." You let go of the memories of the preprogrammed past.

The Way You Perceive, You Create

Your subconscious is functioning directly through the universal cosmic intelligence, where all functions are carried out by the polarity, and opposites are in harmonious co-creation. But the self-conscious ego-mind is in an evolutionary stage that manifests energy frequencies in human beings.

The self-conscious that operates through the medium of the ego-mind vibrates in a frequency that dominates the self-conscious. Whatever you think, either consciously or unconsciously, begins to be automatically translated into your biological feeling center. The self-conscious ego-mind operates through the individually induced frequencies that dominate the cosmic energy field in your body. Individual personal thoughts and feelings dominate the impersonal presence of polarity of *Prana* body. When you react to any situation, you are converting the subconscious frequency of *Prana* body into your personal unconscious karma body, which has a totally different frequency. The karma body manifests through the prepro-

grammed personal past conditioning, which emerges
through the unconscious. Subconscious, self-conscious,
and unconscious are all different frequencies. If you
want to change what is unconscious, you have to go to
the witness of superconscious, which observes all that
is surfacing from the past into the present in the form
of reaction. When you don't identify with reaction, by
not reacting to it, you simply remain witness to all the
reactive thoughts that are passing by. In this way, you
dismantle your preprogrammed unconscious past,
which can be accomplished through meditation.

The Frequencies of the Self

Healing happens with innate intelligence of the
body. Mind and matter are different frequencies of
the eternal Self. The way you interpret the unified
field theory is the way you create your world of experiences. If interpretations are from a sense of separated
self, you set up separation from the source. When you
stop interpreting, you experience the unified field of
consciousness directly. This is perception through the
unconditional witness. You must also act from a constant remembrance that you are divine— not deficient,
lonely, or undeserving. If your perception changes
to that of a higher state of consciousness, you create.

Then, instead of seeing to believe, you can believe to see. You are the seer that creates the scenery. When you change to self-sourcing, you are no longer in the state of object referral that is separated. Rather, there is inner integration.

Meditation Invites Stillness

Meditation is the gateway to choiceless witness. By observing everything within your field of perception with non-reactivity, you dismantle problems and enter into an awareness of what is as is. In this way, you take a quantum leap from reactive interactions of what is present to non-reactive choiceless awareness.

This non-reactive way of being is living in the "fire." It takes great courage, discipline, and practice to sit still and surrender. The quiet approach to constantly alternating positive and negative experiences is the ultimate, invincible defense. Sitting in that fire, you experience the real surrender of ego. When the ego burns, grace showers. You are taken to the unified field of all creativity known as self-sourcing. In this surrendered state, all evolutionary expressions and actions spontaneously and effortlessly emerge. In this grace, your highest desires are fulfilled without having to strive for them. Such desires are founded not in separative consciousness but in the field of unity and integration. When intelligence is rooted in this field of consciousness, you are grounded in self-sourcing and can act with maximum creativity and efficiency. The action itself is self-fulfilling, rather than the end result. Instead of reaction, there is only reality.

Quantum Zero Stress Meditation Achieves Choiceless Witness

When Buddha taught meditation techniques, he created methods for the people of his time who did not suffer from the intense mental and emotional agitation or restlessness that are experienced today. Buddha's simple techniques—witnessing the breath in and out and the movement of the abdomen up and down—were fine for people in 400 BC but are not effective enough for the mind of the 21st century. Today's civilization is in deep distress. The Integrative Amrit Method (I AM) technique of Quantum Zero Stress Meditation is specifically designed to provide an effective technique for today's challenges. It helps an individual find the path of immediate reconnection to the source. The I AM technique allows a practitioner to take a quantum leap before even entering witness consciousness.

Modern-day meditators complain they have too much noise in their heads, due to the mind's chatter and distractions. They cannot reach the silence of witness consciousness. In the I AM process, your mind dissolves and disappears into the energy body. You become so absorbed in the non-mental dimension of non-doing that witness doesn't struggle. You just witness the disturbances that arise internally from reactive mental activity or through the external disturbances. The more your mind dissolves into the energy body, the deeper you move toward the zero stress meditative zone. Even a new meditator can experience integration through this technique.

The purpose of introducing this quantum-breath entry into meditation is not to change any meditation technique you might be doing. Rather, it is intended to enhance whatever you are practicing, to dramatically increase your capacity to drop into deeper levels of meditation with effortless ease. This is a technique that can be used in many different situations and challenges that you encounter in everyday life, from intimate relationships to business interactions. You can adjust the method regardless of where you are, whom you are with, or what you are doing. Use it when you need to focus yourself and tune into your creative life force.

The more you practice, the more effective it will be. You can use it before you go for an interview, perform on stage, take a test, or enter an important meeting. It will increase your clarity of vision, and your effectiveness will soar.

Stop Your Thoughts

Take a moment right now to try an experiment. Set a timer to go off in five minutes. For those five minutes, close your eyes and just be witness to your thoughts, without judging them or engaging in any stories. Let your thoughts just come and go, floating by like clouds in the sky. If you can, drop into the gaps between your thoughts and just be silent. The timer will alert you to the end of the time, so you need not even think about time. Just empty your mind, relax, and be still.

When the timer sounds, ask yourself a few questions. How did the experiment work for you? Did you find yourself wondering how much time had elapsed along the way? Were thoughts creeping in about what you might need to be doing? Were you fidgety? Did some problem surface in your mind and steal your attention? Or were you able to completely let go and be present in the moment? Were you able to remain still? Don't worry if you weren't able to stay fully present. It takes practice, and you will have future opportunities to fine-hone your skills. For now, just briefly write down your experiences.

Thoughts Are Powerful Forms

Thoughts grounded in the past contain the power to bring back old reactions that are not necessarily appropriate for what is being experienced now. For example, if you sit down to a meal and see a dish that reminds you of a previous dinner, you may have expectations before you taste it. Your thoughts tell you it will have just a certain taste or texture, and you become primed for that. When you put the first bite into your mouth and discover it's not the same dish at all, your memory of the past experience may negate the present. You may spend the moment complaining instead of savoring the flavor of the different but well-prepared meal before you. Instead of trying to recreate what was, let go of it and bring your focus back to what is on your plate right now!

Be Present With What Is

Living in the present moment means letting go of that which is either dead or unborn and accepting what exists. It is acceptance of yourself for who you are and where you are. The greater your self-acceptance, the less need you have to strive for something different. You let go of self-rejection. You have more freedom to be who you really are, without projections or escaping into imagination.

When you recognize that you are just part of the natural laws of nature, existing within this context of the universe, you can let go and just be. You are but a drop of water in the ocean of humanity and beyond. Accept and know that you are just a part of the universe rather than struggling to change or alter the natural flow.

An old fable about a group of ants floating on a log down a river illustrates the point dramatically. This group of insects is flowing at breakneck speed down the river, carried along swiftly on the water's surface by the force of the current. The leading ant at the front of the log announces with assurance that he is in control and at the helm, when in fact he has just been caught in the river's current. He might feel like he is in control, since the log is moving with effortless ease and the direction is acceptable. When you move in alignment with the natural forces, you cease to struggle, and life just flows. If the ants had been attempting to go upstream, they would have battled the river, and they may not have survived.

Review of Prana Body

When you shift from thinking to feeling, you find the secret of restoring your connection to life that happens through the medium of *Prana* or energy body. As discussed in earlier chapters, *Prana* is the medium for you to experience life through the feeling center. Everything—all the pleasures and the pain—comes through the feeling of *Prana* body.

Ancient masters found *Prana* to be the most powerful link that connects to the invisible power that cannot be reached, understood, or explained through the mind. That power that resides within you is called the presence. That presence is omnipresent, omniscient, and omnipotent. It is the invisible, undifferentiated presence that you are, which begins to manifest through the differentiated power of polarity, where opposites are in co-creation. Through the I AM techniques, the two powers—the consciousness and the energy—that are separated through the thinking center are brought back together through harmonious interplay in the feeling center.

Linking to the visible power of polarity of *Prana* in your body, you use that as a powerful connection to the invisible, non-mental, spiritual part of you. Once you withdraw from the thinking center by remaining witness to the passing thoughts and feelings, you instantly make a transition from self-conscious to the combined power of superconscious and subconscious. When you have withdrawn and emptied your mind of time-bound past to where it is connected, your body turns into a temple and your heart into a sanctuary for the light of the soul to radiate and transform every cell in your body. In this way, you can heal your body and make it more powerful and more readied for self-realization.

The moment you make a transition from thinking to feeling, you have made a quantum leap from the limited, linear field of the ego-mind into the unlimited power of the *Prana* being. Once you are integrated into your energy body, you enter a subconscious energy level. In this dimension, you are not separate from the cosmic energy body, and you instantly enter into an exponentially expanded state of being. Your *Prana* body is as eternal and timeless as your spirit being. The more often you merge into *Prana*, the longer you can stay there. The less you live in the ego-mind, the more creative, efficient, and effective you become.

Yogi Amrit Desai

Chapter 7

The Secrets of Quantum Breath Meditation

Meditation. The very word invokes scenes of serenity and tranquility, beckoning one to a mystical place of awareness, sensitivity, and all knowing. But how many actually reach that state during hours of sitting on cushions?

The mind is the most difficult thing to harness. In a single hour, your brain processes some 2,000 thoughts. How challenging it is to sit and simply observe those myriad thoughts without becoming involved in a mental dialogue about them. Your legs invariably begin to ache, your skin itches, and you become totally dissatisfied with your performance, judging yourself for your inability to sit still for a half-hour, a quarter-hour, or even for five minutes!

An Excellent Route Into the Zero Stress Zone

Quantum Breath Meditation in the Integrative Amrit Method (I AM) is the master key to unlocking the entry point to the Zero Stress Zone. It allows you to experience a profound paradigm shift that effortlessly silences the mind and draws you into the innermost core of your being. It allows you to disengage the trapped energy in the unconscious that is acting as a dysfunctional emotional reaction. Once this energy is freed from the preprogrammed karmic body of the past, you create a shift from its psychological time-bound unconscious patterns into the subconscious cosmic body that operates with its innate cosmic intelligence. This skill becomes a powerful tool for initiating all forms of miraculous self-healing processes on physical, mental, and emotional levels. It becomes transformational. Silence is the metabolism of immortality, which exists beyond space and time.

The I AM yoga is unique among most meditation techniques. Most start with being witness, where the meditator witnesses with mindful awareness. Unfortunately, many who start meditating this way spend a long time overcoming the physical and mental distractions they encounter. They get absorbed in the discomfort of sitting in a certain position or overwhelmed by their restless mind that permeates their awareness. The result is often an almost painful preoccupation with all the distractions that arise. Failing to use the "witness" aspect effectively leads to discouragement and frustration. Many end up abandoning meditation altogether, because it just seems too difficult.

Third-Eye Focus

Quantum Breath Meditation uses a breath technique with a Third-Eye focus, allowing the meditator to create a quantum leap from the surface disturbances to drop into the Zero Stress Zone effortlessly. When you focus your attention on the Third Eye—your brow center, in the middle of your forehead between your eyebrows—you enter into the higher integrative center of choiceless awareness, where the polarity of left and right brain, sympathetic and parasympathetic, *inga* and *pingala nadi,* sun and moon, inhalation and exhalation unite in harmonious co-creative interplay. It establishes a powerful communion with your divine presence. It illuminates and activates all the brain centers. Every time the brain centers are lit up with *Prana*, you erase the impressions registered in your primitive brain center that acts as fight-or-flight reactions. This is where all healing happens.

This brain center, the amygdala—a subcortical brain structure—is an almond-shaped set of neurons located deep in the brain's medial temporal lobe. It is shown to play a key role in the processing of emotions (in humans and in animals) linked to both fear responses and pleasure. When you combine in-depth relaxation (through alpha and theta brain waves) with meditation, you create a potent combination, producing powerful results.

Whenever you want to change any self-defeating physical, mental, or emotional habits, focusing on the Third Eye will actualize your intentions, affirmations, and prayers from the power of the source within you. In deep meditation, when your mind has totally merged and melted into the energy body, your focus detaches you from all negative moods and emotions.

The consciousness that lights up the brain centers cannot be reached through the mind. In order to erase the preprogrammed past registered in your primitive karma body, you must enter the integrated state of the Third Eye. Only choiceless awareness takes you from the preprogrammed personal past, allowing you entry into the sacred space of your higher centers of integration. Through integration, you find yourself completely dissolving and disappearing into oneness. This oneness is very much like when you enter a deep sleep and do not know that you are asleep. The union you experience as you sleep is called subconscious union. The union that you enter through the meditation technique is through the union of superconscious and subconscious.

In this way, you use your *Prana* body as a link to meditation rather than trying to tackle the distractions that arise—on physical, mental, and emotional levels—in the initial stage of meditation. The moment you enter the witness state, you disengage from the preprogrammed reactive choices and detach from the ego-mind. You withdraw from the doer in the dimension of time, and your whole body—your whole being—enters into a timeless meditative zone. You relax in the present, rather than hoping to relax when you are more experienced and advanced in your meditation practice.

This approach has proved to be so effective that first-time novices can be profoundly moved by their experiences. Even veteran meditators, who have practiced for decades, discover that, during the very first time of using the I AM techniques, they overcome the initial stage of disturbances more easily than ever before and are able to drop into an even deeper state of meditation effortlessly. Regardless of what meditation technique you are now practicing—or even if you are not practicing any—you can easily incorporate the Quantum Breath Meditation and find amazing progress as you enter the depth of meditation more easily.

Two-Winged Approach

Quantum Breath Meditation uses the posture of consciousness with its two-winged approach from doing to being. The practice of doing the technique with integrated intention delivers you into the oneness of being. The transition occurs from the dynamic doing part of meditation to the merging or passive part of non-doing, choiceless witness. In this method, the transition happens almost instantaneously. In the active wing, the dynamic practice creates the ideal condition for the mind to merge into the energy field. As a result, the energy becomes a link to the state of being that activates and raises the frequency of the energy body to a very high level, which instantly drowns the mental and emotional agitations and physical tensions. This alters the usual mind-body conflict. It teaches you how to raise the energy field to such a high intensity that the mind can easily merge and get impregnated into the whole body, into the energy body. The mental body and physical body become impregnated by choiceless awareness that allows your entire being to become deeply absorbed into this state of meditation. In this way, you transcend progressively towards the Zero Stress Zone. The technique promotes deeper integration, inner harmony, and balance, as you take a leap into the non-doing being that you are.

Understanding Mindfulness

When you enter *mindful meditation,* the choiceless state of awareness, you instantly withdraw from all mentally induced activities. In the practice of I AM Yoga, there is a practice of *matyhara* or inward focus. This technique leads to the transition that creates a quantum leap into truly "being" in meditation. The focus from *doing* to *being* is what creates the quantum leap. Meditation is a process on a path that allows you to jump into non-doing, into the authentic being that you are.

The Quantum Breath Meditation provides a powerful entry into the Zero Stress Zone, in the shortest period of time and with the least amount of effort. You may experience joy as you enter a place where your mind is so calm and peaceful, while your body is deeply relaxed. By focusing on the Third Eye, you are automatically drawn into the integrative state of meditative experience.

Quieting the Mind by Raising the Energy Field

This ancient, mystical meditation technique allows you to more easily shift from the ego-mind to a no-conflict miraculous zone. Instead of operating in a place of conflict resolution full of tension, you feel peaceful. Your body turns into a temple, your heart into an altar, and you connect with the timeless presence of your true self.

The Timeless Zone

In this meditation, all mental agitations become silent. Breath activates the energy field and creates the ideal condition for the mind to melt and merge into the energy body. It is always paradoxical that you are doing and not doing. It is a seamless merging of the doing and non-doing, balancing active and receptive, doing and being, making it happen and letting happen.

As the doer and achiever in the dimension of space and time, the ego-mind takes a back seat, and you enter the timeless meditative zone, the stillness that leads to seeing who you truly are. Once your energy body is impregnated with the power of the omnipresent presence of the timeless being, you enter the witness mode, and your bodily functions are disengaged from your time-bound ego-mind. Your autonomic nervous system becomes tuned into the timeless being and functions more optimally in balance and alignment.

The Restless Meditator

Some people can enter meditation like a seasoned practitioner, but some, struggling with restlessness or lack of focus, may get frustrated quickly. The solution is to develop a consistent practice and challenge yourself to a commitment over a period of time. Establish appropriate preparations to reinforce a behavioral conditioning that sets your body and mind to desire the meditative experience. For instance, successful writers and authors discover that, by sitting in front of their computers at the same time every day for several hours, they condition their minds to function more freely, opening the channels of inspiration. They may have days when no words flow, but on other days, they are a fountain of ideas. By setting the process in motion, the muse is more likely to appear. Of course, some days will be more productive than others, and even that is part of the whole experience.

Practicing this technique every day at the same time can make a significant impact, but even if you miss once, continue to integrate it in your day whenever possible. If the space is available in your house, create a special room or area for your meditation practice and create a surrounding that is conducive to relaxing. Make it cheerful so that, every time you approach, a shift in your energy is activated. This provides you with a head-start on the process. As much as possible, keep that area as a place where you can read and reflect on self-observation and self-study. Keep a journal or reflect on your day's events, re-evaluating and re-structuring your behavior patterns so that you have adopted an active re-visitation and bring it into alignment with your meditative mode of being.

Learning to Let Go Consciously

In meditation, your *Prana* body becomes the portal to access the superconscious state of being that you are. Most people who try to meditate but don't know how to use this subtle *Prana* body as the link to the superconscious have a hard time entering into the non-mental dimension, and the meditative state becomes elusive. When you are engaged by thought forms, you are shaping life through these thought forms that you create, and your experiences of life continue to be perceived through your mind. Once you learn how to disengage from the thinking center, you can accomplish the quieting of the mind more easily. In this system, you learn how to activate your energy field through the breath, so that your body becomes the pulsating energy field, where every cell in your body is lit up with consciousness. The transition from thinking to feeling then becomes much easier, allowing you to let your mind dissolve completely in the pulsating energy field.

The uniqueness of this technique is that, instead of using witness consciousness to silence the mind, you use "feeling." This approach absolves the mind and dissolves its restlessness instantly. It creates a powerful entry into meditation. This is often the stumbling point where many meditators struggle for days or months—sometimes, years—to enter this state. In the next section of this chapter, you'll learn the primary form of this technique, so that you can begin to use it in your life. You can experience the power and success that comes with it. Of course, more advanced techniques are also available, but they must be taught by specially trained I AM teachers.

In chapter 4, you were given an experience that incorporated one of the most life-changing breathing techniques. It immediately transforms your reaction into response, to allow you to face and dismantle any challenge. A simple ancient yogic breathing technique, this is at the core of the Level One Quantum Breath

Meditation; in just one minute, it can transform a tense moment into a moment of peace and tranquility. It can help you unravel and release stress from its very source.

Entering the Zero Stress Zone

The Quantum Breath Meditation

Quantum Breath Meditation is designed to pro-gressively take you to subtler and deeper levels of integration. To achieve the most benefit from your first experience, you may record the directions and listen to your recording as you follow the procedures. Alterna-tively, read the technique thoroughly and then let go into the experience, without worrying about whether or not you are doing the technique exactly right. Let go of judgment and just allow yourself to feel the experience. Whatever you remember will be what is right for you to start with, so just trust the process. For subsequent sessions, you can re-read the technique and check it against your perception of what you're doing. Remem-ber that the intention is to drop into a place of non-do-ing, of allowing yourself just to be, without mental agita-tions or judgments. Start slowly and relax with whatever the experience is for your first time. The purpose of all meditation techniques is to return back to the infinite source of energy, power, and information that is hidden within you, to connect to the "I am that I am."

The Quantum Breath Meditation provides an essential experience that can change your life. Take your time to review this section; read through it several times before implementing it for yourself. Make sure you are completely comfortable with the process and review the precautions. Preparations should include:

- Practicing at the same time every day.
- Choosing an appropriate place that's your special or sacred place.
- Wearing comfortable clothing.
- Giving yourself permission to devote a certain period of time, whether it's just a few minutes or a longer period of time.

Most of all, practice routinely, until it becomes habitual, like brushing your teeth.

Instructions for the Practice

Ideally, practice for 30 minutes twice daily, starting at sunrise or early morning and repeating in late afternoon. When you awake in the morning, you are usually closest to your natural energy center. In fact, at sunrise, the sun's energy is at its highest tide, which is the most powerful and invigorating of energies.

The most benefit occurs between 4:00 a.m. and 6:30 a.m. Experiment with it for yourself—but whatever you choose, be consistent. You may also practice the technique any time you feel fatigued, anxious, stressed, worried, or fearful. You will notice its power to free you from self-defeating emotional reactions with even 5 or 10 minutes of practice, any time during the day.

During the entire breathing meditation practice, keep your attention focused on the Third Eye. Maintain the tip of your tongue touching the roof of your mouth, just behind the upper teeth.

Preparation Guidelines for Level One Quantum Breath Meditation

Before you begin, wash your face, feet, and hands. Use a few yoga postures or stretch your body to release any stiffness and tensions that you might be feeling. Select a comfortable seated position and sit up straight. Maintain an erect spine during the entire practice. As you sit, notice if you feel the energy moving up your spine and out the crown of your head. If you can't, don't give it another thought. Notice what you are feeling. You can sit on the floor or on a cushion; if you use a chair, position your feet flat on the floor.

Recite aloud the following *Asatoma* prayer to center yourself and set an intention for your practice:

- Lead me from unreality to reality.
- Lead me from darkness to light.
- Lead me from time-bound consciousness to the time-transcendent being that I am.

Take a few slow, deep breaths. Observe your breath as it contracts and expands your body. Bring your fingertips gently to your eyelids and place your palms in contact with your face. Take a deep breath and breathe out with a sigh. Notice the feeling of your touch: skin on skin. Very slowly and gently, massage areas of your face, starting with the forehead, and moving on to the eyebrows, temples, jaws, eyes, etc. Feel all tension melt away under the healing touch of your fingers and palms. Finally, place your fingertips gently back on your eyelids with both palms flat, touching and covering your entire face. Take a deep breath in and exhale, releasing any tensions and expectations. Repeat three deep breaths; on the third exhalation, allow your hands to float into your lap, on your knees, or wherever they feel comfortable.

Special Breath Technique

With your eyes closed, begin the "Straw" breathing: take a full, deep inhalation through your nose, filling your lungs with vital life force energy; then blow the air out through gently pursed lips, as if blowing through a straw. The exhalation is to be extended and prolonged as much as possible. As the exhalation begins to become thinner and finer towards the end, focus your attention on the Third Eye. After each breath, rest in complete stillness, focused in the Third Eye, and drop into the feeling center by bringing all your undivided attention to feeling the energy field activated by the breath. By entering the feeling so completely, you allow your attention to be totally absorbed in the feeling center, so that there is nothing happening on the level of the mind. When you focus your attention on the Third Eye, you are lifting and attracting energy to it. Remember, energy follows attention.

With choiceless awareness, feel the energetic impact of breath felt in the form of sensations in your body. Let your awareness descend into your body, dropping into your *Prana* or energy body. You may feel the intensified sensations and presence of *Prana* in the form of surging waves, ripples of energetic pulsations, upward spiraling, tingling, and/or heat. You may notice sensations or thoughts. Just allow them to pass through, without engaging or judging them. Remain witness, the observer of thoughts, feelings, or sensations that may arise. If you become distracted, focus on the breath to re-engage yourself in stillness. If you feel nothing, just notice that.

With each exhalation, feel the release of tension, anxiety, and fear. Proceed very slowly and mindfully. As you breathe out, let go, releasing anything that no longer serves you, including old energies and toxins. As you inhale, breathe in joy and love and let the vibrational frequencies of love permeate your entire body—every muscle, every nerve, every cell. Repeat this form of breathing seven or more times; then sit in complete silence. Allow the breath to return naturally. Witness how you feel.

With practice, your eyes may naturally converge upward toward the Third Eye. Maintain focus on the Third Eye with intense alertness and notice any bodily felt sensations. Just let go and be present. Stay in this meditation for as long as feels right to you.

After you've finished, take a moment to write down how you feel. Make brief notes for yourself so that you can quantify how you feel afterwards. It will serve to help you be more mindful of the experience.

At the conclusion, notice your breath pattern and whether or not it is soft, almost imperceptible. Notice how relaxed your body is and how it is reflected in the form of a calm mind. Practice, practice, practice.

When you re-enter into activity of your day, notice the difference in the way you interact with the people you meet, situations you encounter, and places you visit. All day long, keep that record. The most important part is to pay attention to the difference this meditation is making in your interpersonal relationships and the manner in which you handle challenges you face in life.

Important Precautions

As with any practice, experiment for yourself and be mindful of any health concerns or restrictions you may have. Please note the following:

1. If you have low blood pressure, this breathing technique can lower it more. Be cautious.

2. If you feel dizzy or light-headed, stop the practice immediately and continue normal breathing.

Different Experiences

There is no right or wrong experience. You may experience very different sensations on any given day.

Here are just a few of the experiences people have had while doing this meditative technique:

- Spectacular spectrum of colors
- Single color or no color, just blackness or white
- Swirls of images and textures
- Pulsations in the body
- Jerking sensations
- Echoing sounds
- Visions
- Hot or cold sensations in different parts of the body
- Nothing (emptiness)
- Overwhelming sense of joy
- Tears streaming for no apparent reason

Practice. Practice. Practice.

The more you practice the Quantum Breath Zero Meditation, the more you will want to do it, because it will deepen your connection to the power of presence that you are. You will develop a sense of integrity, self-confidence, and spontaneous and joyous participation in life situations. This inner source of oneness is the fundamental source of love and compassion. As it begins to grow, you—and people you encounter in your daily life—will notice that you carry a bubble of energy, of love and compassion. It will create an energetic, non-mental, synergistic communion to others everywhere you go—in everything you do and with everyone you meet.

Colors of Meditation

I've been practicing the breath meditation. This time was very interesting. Often, when I begin, I want to focus upon the breath. So sometimes and even today, I was becoming preoccupied with breath at first and I would say "go to the Third Eye"—and somewhere along the line, I lost the breath. I ignored the breath and sank in through the Third Eye. And often I see the colors. Purple. Looks like water. Wavy. But a beautiful purple. But this time it was funny, because I often see an eyeball blinking at me. But this time there was a little guy, and he was blue. There was a wavy kind of veil, a purple veil, and he kind of peeked through and blinked his eye. And it amused me, and I became joyful and light of spirit. I felt all of a sudden that I had become weightless.

—Trish, Philadelphia, Pennsylvania

Chapter 8

Understanding How Meditation Can Renew Your Life

By setting a daily routine of stilling your body and mind, you can find more solutions in your life where before you saw only problems. The effects take place on a non-mental level, as you allow your energies to flow smoothly in a balanced, peaceful way. Modern research and scientific tests have shown meditative techniques create a marked change in the pattern of brain waves, which can produce long-term healing effects. As a result, many physicians have started recommending meditation for a variety of illnesses, chronic disorders, and pain. The benefits occur in three essential categories: psychological, physiological, and spiritual.

Physical and Psychological Benefits

Studies indicate that, with daily meditation, longevity may be enhanced by 5 to 12 years. Electroencephalogram (EEG) studies demonstrate the increase of alpha brain waves during meditation; these are directly linked to relaxation of the nervous system. Stress hormones are reduced, blood pressure and heart rate declines, and the metabolic system slows down. Activating the pineal gland secretes melatonin, which helps to prevent illness, retard premature aging, induce more restful sleep, boost the immune system, and promote healing.

When you completely let go into a deeply relaxed state of being, the brain and entire nervous system rest and restore. The following physical effects have been noted:

- The body's metabolism is lowered.
- Heart rate is lowered.
- The autonomic nervous system restores the balance between tension and relaxation.
- Blood pressure is reduced. For those suffering from high blood pressure or stress-related disorders (such as anxiety, fatigue, insomnia, and depression), the benefits are impactful. If you are taking medication, you'll need to closely monitor your dosages, as the need for them may be reduced.

- Cholesterol levels are reduced, which can help prevent cardiovascular diseases, heart attacks, or strokes.
- The damaging effects of stress-released cortisol are reduced, and less of the chemical is released into the bloodstream.

Psychological benefits can also accrue. Deep relaxation can:

- Elevate mood and a sense of self-confidence, integrity, and dignity by immediately improving self-image.
- Dramatically reduce levels of anxiety, depression, and quality of sleep as brain-wave patterns improve.
- Bring an integrated state of being. When mind, body, and heart work in harmony, you may experience ecstasy.
- Create shifts in compulsive behaviors, thoughts, and emotions, giving you amazing freedom to live life as a celebration.
- Free the trapped energy and accelerate inner healing processes. It generates a renewed energy level that brings a sense of vitality, strength, and courage to face life's challenges with equanimity.

- Accelerate healing processes to bring renewal and rejuvenation.
- Increase your happiness quotient and provide you with improved emotional stability. The process allows you to open up, so that energy flows more creatively. For many artists and performers, this brings inspiration.
- Liberate the wisdom of the body to carry out self-healing and transformative processes from within.

Even as your body continues to grow old, you can maintain youthful spirit—vitality and enthusiasm—that never gets old with the aging body. The more you stay connected to your energy body, the more you increase the natural immunity of your body to fight off infections, inflammation, and premature aging.

Spiritual Benefits

Meditation escorts you into a deeper realization of your Self. In the process, there is a merging and blending into the oneness of your divine essence, the being who you are. As you drop into stillness, you:

- Experience more harmony in everything you do.
- See peacefulness, where before you saw conflict.

- Bring balance, where before you had stress.
- Increase capacity to perceive the external world of objects as a mirror that reveals everything (that had been invisible) as imbalances within you.
- See every interaction as the self-observation and self-study where all changes you were seeking from others or outside yourself are manifested from within.
- Discover that solutions to problems you were seeing from others or outside are coming from within you.
- Feel a new sense of mastery of life.
- Release fear of old age, sickness, and death, as you become more connected to your *Prana* body.
- Experience the shift of mind that has been acting as a tool of ego and observe it transform into a powerful tool of consciousness.
- Live in inner harmony, which automatically dismantles the defensive mode previously encountered in interactions with others.
- See the increase in acceptance, love, and recognition that you sought from others now revealing itself from within and being reflected by everyone you meet.

Extending the Effects of Meditation Into Your Daily Activities

In order to extend your meditation practice into your everyday life, here are some mindful suggestions:

1. Wherever you are, be there fully.
2. Whatever you are doing, do it totally.
3. Whomever you are with, accept them unconditionally.
4. Enter now from whatever you are doing.
5. Enter now from wherever you are.
6. Enter now from your conditioned past.
7. Take complete responsibility for what you are feeling.

As you enter your meditative practices and lifestyle, always give more attention to being grateful for all the wonderful changes that you are experiencing. Withdraw completely from complaining about things that you have not yet worked through. Once you follow this guidance, your practice will progress, and commitment will grow. Results will follow.

One-Step Turnaround

Another way to extend your meditative awareness into your daily life is with the Bean Game. Carry some beans (or beads) in your pocket. Start with 21 beans in your left pocket. Each time you become aware that you are having a reaction and are able to successfully dismantle it by withdrawing your reaction, you enter into a "turnaround" technique. You create a conscious shift—from attention and energy moving into the habitual ways and patterns of reactions—and turn it into nonreactive awareness. Once you make this turnaround, take one bean from your left pocket and put it in your right pocket; this symbolically represents irrational, reactive, logical left brain transitioning to insightful, creative opening of the right brain. In this way, you access the higher power to handle challenges. If, at the end of the day, you have 21 beans in your right pocket, you made amazing progress, as this process will register as a shift from left brain to right brain, to the nonreactive, intuitive dimension. The turnaround technique is a constructive creative resolution to any challenge you face in your life.

From a scientific perspective, this process helps to create new, more positive neural pathways in the brain. In the neurosciences, brain plasticity is shown to be cultivated through mindful changes in patterns of behavior. As you become more aware of your fight-or-flight responses from stress-producing thoughts, activities, or situations, you can train in ways that change the impact of the stress response on your mind and body. You can actually reduce the impact of cortisol and other stress hormones. As soon as you are aware that your heart is racing or your breathing is increasing, you can use a one-step turnaround technique to change that behavioral response.

Without abatement, stress actually impacts changes in the amygdala, which in turn affects the hippocampus (the memory center); that, in turn, can interfere with the neural pathways to the prefrontal cortex, which is the CEO of the brain—the place for decision making and reasoning. Over time, if stress is nonstop, the brain actually shrinks, and neural connections are seriously impaired. However, the plasticity of the brain allows for changes and adaptations to be made that can actually expand its capacity. Countless scientific research projects have now verified the benefits of expanding brain function through meditation, yoga, and Yoga Nidra.

Transforming Energy With a One-Step Turnaround

Ordinarily, all unconscious patterns that are built into the karmic body of self-image are preprogrammed to move attention and energy downward and outward through the first three *chakras* or energy centers. The root, sacral, and solar plexus *chakras* represent survival, sensuality, and power centers; these function and operate in the external world for the sustenance, survival, health, and well-being of both the body and the body of the self-image with which you identify. The Turnaround game described previously offers a technique of withdrawal. *Pratyahara* is an integral part of *Ashtanga* Yoga and represents the turning around of attention, driven by the ego-mind in a downward and outward mode of reactive action. When you practice withdrawing your attention from the reactive choices of *for* or *against* to choiceless awareness, you are turning around from the energy moving downward and outward to it moving inward and upward, towards the heart and the higher energy centers of integration.

The purpose of turnaround is to release the trapped energy from self-destructive modes to a more integrated state of being. It transforms the energy.

The Amazing Power of Breath

Your first breath occurs as you are born into the world. Your last breath is expelled as you die. Breath is the essence of life and affects virtually every part of the body. It oxygenates the body, revitalizes organs, muscles, tissues, and cells, and discharges toxins. You might imagine that most of the body's toxins would be released through defecation, urination, and sweat. In fact, the human body is designed to discharge 70% of the toxins through breathing. The bottom line is that breath fuels energy production, improves focus and concentration, strengthens the immune system, reduces stress and anxiety, increases feelings of calmness, lowers blood pressure, and more.

Your Breath Reflects Your Mood

Your breath is a barometer of how you're feeling at any given moment in time. When you're angry or anxious, your breath will be short, quick, and shallow, which is typically accompanied by elevated blood pressure. When you're relaxed, your breath is a steady, rhythmic stream. Even watching a suspenseful movie or an upsetting news clip can induce a change in your breathing, to a heightened, shortened breath.

The most mind-boggling aspect of this reality is that you can change how you're feeling by changing your breathing. A powerful way to jump-start any change in almost any situation is to focus on your breathing. Whenever you want to change any self-defeating thoughts or reactive behavior, just take a full, deep breath.

To heighten the calming effects of breathing, use the Straw Breathing technique as outlined in the Quantum Breath Meditation in chapter 7. This ancient yogic *Pranayama* has a tranquilizing effect on the entire nervous system and cleanses toxins from the body. It reduces stress, neutralizes the fight-or-flight response, and lowers blood pressure.

Practice daily—even for just a short time—so the method becomes second nature and automatic. When you feel a sudden flush of anxiety, frustration, anger, or illness, you'll be prepared to stop for a moment and change the feeling with your breathing. Some people do it in their cars when traffic becomes frustrating (but don't do it if you're in the driver's seat); others use it to perform more effortlessly, whether on stage or at work. You can do it effectively with your eyes either open or closed.

Shifting From Meltdown

In a recent instance, a group of women were playing a league tennis match in southwest Florida. After more than an hour of playing, one of the players began to experience heart palpitations and, understandably, became frightened as she was consumed with fear and panic. As she sat down, her face turned ghostly white. Her opponent knew Straw Breathing and immediately guided her through the technique, to calm and relax her, and allowing the opponent to assess the situation and the moment. In just three minutes of breathing, the woman was restored to feeling perfectly fine and, within another 10 minutes, actually continued and finished the tennis match.

In another instance, a young mother burst into uncontrollable tears for no apparent reason. She didn't know what to do or how to regain her composure as she continued sobbing. Once again, Straw Breath came to the rescue. In just minutes of following the technique, the young woman felt completely in control and in the zone.

During a business program in which Straw Breath was taught to a group of employees, one of the young men confessed at the end of the series that this technique had changed his life with his family. He has made it a routine that, every day when he comes home from work, he sits for five minutes and uses this breathing technique before engaging in the evening activities. He claims this process has given him patience, calmness, and a much more joyful atttitude, as well as more quality time with his family.

People who have used this breath technique have reported that they were able to reduce anxiety, depression, insomnia, and stress levels in just moments. It also helps to support the body's natural healing capabilities.

Self-Healing with Breath

"A couple years ago I had my cervical spine x-rayed and found that my C2 and C3 were fused together and had been my whole life, crushing my brain stem and making me legally disabled from pain and illness. I decided to truly apply myself to separating those two bones and healing my neck. Well, after the Quantum Breath weekend, I was at a fair and they offered free spinal exams, so I got another x-ray. Miracle of miracles, my C2 and C3 are two separate bones with normal appearance. I know from other experiences that flowing *Prana* through the body can and does perform miracles in the matter of the body. That experience on top of the weekend opened me to a new level of practicing with confidence that it is working. I am not perfect at flowing the *Prana*, but it is my passion as a yoga practice."

—Christa Rose, Boulder, Colorado

Chapter 9

Anxiety and Fear Begone

Your life is suspended in the continuum of time. You are constantly moving from yesterday towards tomorrow. Yesterday becomes only a memory of the past, and tomorrow is still a dream of what may come. Yet today, the Now, is the only time in which you are truly living. It is your authentic experience. Once you have experienced it, it too fades into memory, and you enter a new moment of life that you call the present. The present is filled with a myriad of thoughts. All thought forms arise out of reactions to the present and are part of your personal and socially conditioned preprogrammed past. As a result, 99% of the reactive thoughts with which you identify are lying to you about what you see, feel, experience, and interact with in the present.

When fear takes over, it motivates you to try to protect yourself from problems that do not exist. Anxiety is like praying for what you do not want. Anxiety combined with fear takes hold of your energy and turns it against life. Everything you do after that keeps you separated from the other. You become self-centered, tortured by and suffering from loneliness, while you seek love and acceptance from others and objects of entertainment.

Your Thoughts May Be Poison

When you identify with your thoughts, they become reality. When you believe your thoughts to be true, your energy is engaged and creates a chemical shift in your body, giving the thoughts form. They become physical reality and turn into moods, which can be destructive.

Every crisis and conflict that you face at any moment is created by your distorted reactive perception of reality—the problem of the perceiver, not the perceived. When you learn to withdraw your reaction from the perceived and reshape your perception, you eliminate the fundamental problem.

The Science of Restorative Energy Converted to Self-Destruction

As discussed in earlier chapters, whenever you are in reaction, your thought forms take the subconscious

Pranic energy and convert it into distorted perception of reality. As a result, this energy, which is extended and expanded through the reaction, is an unfulfilling experience. The gestalt remains incomplete. The energy connected to the misperception of reality is converted from its subconscious into the unconscious karmic body of the self-image. Every reaction is an emotionally charged psychic weapon to defend the self-image.

All the incomplete experiences that are built into your karmic body of self-image have been built around the Self that you are. Every reaction is aimed against whatever triggers your anger, fear, and jealousy, but it becomes a misdirected war zone, where all the ammunition and weapons are firing at a target that doesn't exist. Whatever you fear and fight against does not have power over you. It is the fear that has the power. The fear feeds your emotional reaction. Once you realize that your reaction is the real problem and it comes within the circle of your influence, you are empowered to create the shift from within. The shift is from reaction to responsive action.

Taking Off the Blinders

Every time you are angry, fearful, or frustrated, a powerful, emotionally charged force flows through you, programmed from the past. For instance, if you were abused or hurt by a bearded man in the past, the reaction that you had in the past is reignited every time you face someone who appears like him. However, this reaction being staged against the person in the present is only a false image that you are fighting. You have lost your capacity to live in the present. As more of these reactive patterns are stored in the body of your person, the more often you will be caught in reaction, fighting with situations that are only the triggers but are not really present. You are fighting phantoms.

Reaction creates a negative loop, generating feedback between the body and mind. Break the loop by intercepting and reversing it in the mental body before it turns into verbal or physical action. When you do not express your reaction, it is often perceived as repression. However, when you practice *pratyahara*—conscious withdrawal from your reaction—you are discharging the reactive chain of thoughts, feelings, and actions. You open a whole new channel for processing the experience consciously.

Change Is Not to Be Feared

Change is the force of destruction but also the force of creation. Underlying opposites is the integration that is inherent in change. Change has neither ups nor downs. It is neither good nor bad, neither right nor wrong. All opposites are polarity, aligned with the laws of nature—light and dark, positive and negative, birth and death. They become one through change.

When you trust change, you are at peace. If you change with the changes, you won't be afraid of the future. Change is timeless. It has no future and no past.

Freedom From Attraction or Repulsion

Change is the reality of the material world, while changelessness is the reality of the spiritual world. Change is based on cause and effect. Changeless spirit has neither cause nor effect. It exists beyond all changes. All changes are inherent in the changeless reality.

Change has no choice or preference and is free from attraction or repulsion. It moves through all opposites unaffected. It is central to harmony and balance between two opposites. Change is how the whole phenomenal world is born, grows and evolves.

You resist change when you experience pleasure, but you want change when you experience pain. You are in a love-hate relationship with the opposing experiences of life that constantly change. You develop all sorts of control systems—through money, power, skills, manipulation, and mind control—to circumvent change. If you have personal attachments or preferences for any given experience—which is bound to change—then you are bound to the fear of change.

Change is impersonal; however, resistance to change is personal. "I want change at the rate I want it, and in the way I want it"—that is personal. Personal desires and impersonal change are in perpetual conflict. Because you are embodied spirit, you have the potential to participate in the physical body and live in the changeless state of consciousness through choiceless awareness. Attachment to either choice or witness is only a human possibility. Witness consciousness is individual, but change is universal. Through witness consciousness, the individual merges into the universal through total trust in change.

The greatest opportunity for transformation as individuals—and as a planet—comes in moments of crisis, which create change. While times of prosperity and stability promote only superficial shifts, crisis shakes the foundation of safety and comfort to which you are accustomed, calling for profound paradigm shifts.

This is an opportunity to seek resolution that doesn't just come from overpowering the external enemy but from revisiting and transforming your own distorted perceptions, dysfunctional belief systems, and personal biases. You can replace them with new ways to live and act from love, light, and compassion.

Acceptance Is Powerful

Imagine if your parents just accepted you 100% the way you are. It would have created a much more relaxed parenting process. They never would have raised their voice to you with disappointment, anger, or emotion, so you would never have developed a defensive mechanism. They would have established an easy communication with you. If you want to change someone, accept them just the way they are. Now, when you communicate as an adult with your children, spouse, friend, or next-door neighbor, just accept them first, before you reject them. Your rejection comes from your preprogrammed past. When you accept unconditionally who you are and who they are, you open a whole new channel of acknowledging what is as is.

When Christ said "Love thy neighbor as thyself," He was speaking of unconditional acceptance of yourself, in order to accept your neighbor unconditionally.

Being Upset on Your Journey

Perfection is not the purpose of these practices. The path is eternal; there is no end. When you practice the meditation for awhile, you might observe: "But I still get upset." The journey is continuous. It's important to remember not to become upset about being upset or angry or irritated. It is part of the human journey. If you have moments of being upset, accept it. You cannot stop someone else from being upset, just as you cannot stop yourself from being upset at a given situation. Accept what is as is and allow it to help you evolve on your path.

Healing Release When Letting Go of Shame and Blame

"I have gone through 59 years of my life shaming and finding fault with myself as well as comparing, judging, and blaming others for my own unhappiness. On Thursday, April 29, 2010, my life was forever changed after listening to [Gurudev's] talk during my *Panchakarma* treatment. As I look back, I have learned more in these past months about myself and life than I did in six years of college and more than 50 years of life's experiences.

"My *Panchakarma* experience was so profound that I wanted to learn as much as possible about the programs offered at the Amrit Yoga Institute. So, I signed up for the Goddess class and experienced another reflective program. After the Goddess class, I was fortunate enough to meet with Gurudev, who told me that I would benefit from the Yoga Teacher's Training Program that was starting in three days. I felt so honored that Gurudev would even consider me for this program since I had little to no yoga experience. So, I signed up and attended Level I teacher's training program.

"Over the summer months, I got up almost every morning at 5:30 a.m. for my two-hour yoga posture practice. Many mornings at 4:15 a.m., I would awake to the sound of Gurudev's voice saying: "Neither choose for or against. Just remain choiceless." These words confirmed that I needed to get up out of bed and do my *asanas*. Little by little, I began to change. Many of the things that seemed important to me before lost importance. I appeared to be more loving and kind, my relationships started to change, and I began to be able to identify external conflicts as an off-the-mat yoga posture.

"On Friday, I visited my doctor for my six-month asthma checkup and to get my blood work for my thyroid disease. When I walked into my doctor's office, the first thing she said to me was, 'You have shifted! You look great!' My exam resulted in a 20-pound weight loss in four months, reduced blood pressure, and no wheezing! She even said that, if I keep doing what I'm doing, then she may be able to take me off of the asthma medicine that I have been taking for the past 15 years! I feel so grateful and humbled for the blessings that I have been given. Thank you my beloved Gurudev for lighting my path!

"Well here I am on this incredible love-filled path. Through your teachings and your loving guidance, I have learned to accept and love myself just as I am at this very moment. Each day, something else unfolds and I am amazed and in love with this journey..."

—L. Altman, Jacksonville, Florida

Chapter 10

Intentions and Affirmations

Without direction, your life will continue to be driven by preprogrammed beliefs, behaviors, and habits. You will be a victim of your own fears and attachments, glued to your self-image through your identification with your thoughts, emotions, opinions, beliefs, likes, and dislikes.

Do you know what you want from life? Until you determine your path with clarity, your guidance system is haphazard. One day you may be spiritual; the next, you may be focused on material things. The ego sets the direction like a seesaw of ups and downs. In order to focus, intention guides you towards fulfillment throughout your journey all along the path, not only when you reach the end. What is desired in the end must be present in the beginning. Mangoes cannot be harvested from planting lemon seeds. Your intention is a seed that must permeate every step and every aspect of your life. All facets of your intention must be directed toward what you say, feel, and do.

Getting From the Beginning What You Want in the End

An intention is a path with only direction: to keep you moving forward. With intention, you walk in the direction you want to walk without impatience to get there and without anxiety about arriving. Intention is the passage that integrates your doing into your being, guiding you on your journey through time to the time-less state of being. This intuitive direction, which is the destiny of the soul, is not to be compromised by any-thing other than its primary purpose. Once you define what you truly want, your identification with it will exert a powerful magnetic force. When you act outside of your intention, you sense a strong pull that realigns with your ultimate intention.

Your intention is your mission statement and defines exactly how you want to experience life. When you make choices in your life that are in alignment with your intention, life flows effortlessly. You are relaxed and absorbed in what you are doing. It is a process of growth, nurturing and watching the seed as it flowers into fulfillment.

Goal Versus Intention

A goal is very different from an intention. A goal has a destination and a measurable endpoint. Goals are useful and often necessary in the physical world. Intention has no endpoint. In the spiritual world, an endpoint is not measurable. Goal orientation creates attachment to an end result, an outcome, and potentially creates conflict between where you are and where you want to be. This generates expectations that induce tension, stress, and anticipation. All goals are searching for something in the external world, which does not work for inner growth. With goals, it is always about such concepts as "When I get there," "When I accomplish something," "When I have a million dollars," and "In the future, I will be happy."

When you set an intention, you are central and present. In a goal, what you *get* is central. An intention anchors your attention, orchestrates your actions, and provides direction for choices in relationships and situations encountered in life. The sources of motivation for meeting a goal and serving an intention are entirely different. With intention, what happens to you in the process is far more important than what you get or when you get it. With an intention, it is the journey. It is the path you set; as long as you are on the path—as long as you are in alignment with your intention—life flows without struggle or tension, and decisions are obvious and more easily made.

Consider that you've set a goal (not an intention) to lose weight. You have a big event coming up, and you want to look your best and fit into a special suit or dress. You decide that you will lose 10 pounds in eight weeks, and you diet to achieve this weight loss. What happens at the end of two months, when there's a good chance that you haven't lost the weight? Typically, the result is a feeling of frustration, disappointment, or even anger, spiced with self-recriminations. "Why didn't I lose it?" It's problematic, as you are attached to the outcome of weight loss and have gone about the process by projecting an endpoint somewhere in the future.

Instead, think about what you truly want. The scenario is to "look your best," but perhaps the underlying motivation is really to find a spouse, to be loved, and to live happily ever after. Looking your best may also suggest feeling your best. How can you feel better every day and not just when you reach some arbitrarily set goal? Will finding a spouse be the key that brings you happiness?

Intention: For External Achievement or Internal Awakening

A primary intention can be used as the foundation for working intentions. The primary intention becomes your life's mission statement, your guiding light, your energetic thoughts that create your reality. Intention becomes a constant reference point: your North Star, keeping you moving in the right direction. An intention should not be defined by wanting to control, manage, or modify external conditions, but rather by wanting to draw strength, power, wisdom, and guidance from the source within. What you experience externally is a direct reflection of what is within.

When you do not have clarity or passion about what you want, it cannot take shape. If your intention is for your own gain, the energy available for it to manifest is limited. It cannot have more than what you already have at your disposal. If it is aligned with spirit, though, it has infinite possibilities.

Working intentions can be used to clear what is blocking the way to fully experiencing your primary intention. Intermediate intentions can be external issues of health, survival, livelihood, and environment. When you are unhealthy, your primary intention is not as keen a focus, because your attention will naturally turn more toward what the body is feeling. The mind resumes control, and survival instincts take over. A working intention can help you get back on track so that your primary intention stays clear and uncompromised. Intermediate intentions must always be in compliance with the primary intention, so you can work through obstacles.

Instead of setting a goal, develop a working intention. In the weight-loss scenario, your intention might be "to eat mindfully and healthfully"—and by doing so, you can feel good every day. Every meal you consume is evolved from your awareness to choose foods that nurture your body, delivering a good balance of vitamins and minerals. Ultimately, you will feel better; quite likely, you will lose weight as the body functions more optimally. Additionally, with more mindfulness about what you choose to eat, you are less likely to eat foods that are not in alignment with making you feel good. You, your mind, and your body will become more attuned to what is harmonious with your well-being.

Your intention must be in total alignment with your feelings and values. If you say one thing but think and feel another, your intention will not be the truth and will not resonate with you. Instead, it will generate more conflict and stress.

You may indeed lose weight and attract a mate, but you may still be unhappy if your weight issues are used to keep a distance in relationships. You may have a conflict with your subconscious part that says you use weight to keep yourself from being hurt. To create a working intention, you must first address the underlying issue about yourself.

In another example, envision yourself in a beautiful house overlooking the beach. You take in the salty smell of the ocean and see waves crashing along the shoreline, the vast stretches of silky white sand, a sprawling spacious beach house, and your friends being lavishly entertained. You feel the pride of ownership. Deep within yourself, though, you feel you don't deserve such a grand place or that you simply can't afford it. The thought becomes a source of conflict and disintegration. To create a viable intention, address your inner feelings of self-worth and issues about prosperity.

Setting an Intention

The most direct route to forming an intention is through meditation. When you quiet the mind and drop into stillness, you open your self to connect to the source within. Allowing yourself a regular practice, in which you release all tension and drop into deep relaxation, unveils your inner truth, your essence, your divine self.

Another method is self-study called *Swadhyaya* in Sanskrit, from Patanjali's collection of Yoga Sutras that guide the authentic practice of yoga. To understand anything in life—as in math, science, music, or medicine—you have to study. Studying yourself is just as important for self-understanding, improvement, and personal growth.

To recognize your primary intention, write down your thoughts. What do you want most in life? Why do you want what you want? What's really important to you? If you're having difficulty identifying or really visualizing what you value, write the names of five or six people you admire. It doesn't matter if they are living or dead. Next to the names, write the qualities you admire about each one. Review the list of qualities and notice which ones are repeated more than once. These should give you some insight into what you value.

An intention should be written in the present tense, expressing what you feel in as few words as possible. Your statement should not be complicated, religious, or moralistic. "Feel" what you are saying. The qualities of an intention should be:

1. Timelessness
2. A direction, not a destination
3. No attachment to an end result
4. No predictable outcome
5. Constant reference point
6. Present tense
7. Concise, precise, and powerful

How to Use Affirmations

Affirmations can be extremely useful in guiding the flow from the inner self. Each day, before stepping out of bed, establish statements for your well-being. Simply affirm that there is nothing in this world that can stop you from transforming your life, opening your heart, loving yourself, and sharing your love with everyone you encounter.

Affirmations are statements of truth that are made in the present. For instance, an affirmation for prosperity that says "I will be wealthy some day" would only reinforce a poverty consciousness because the wealth is deferred to some future point instead of now. A better, more productive affirmation would be to declare: "I am prosperous." An affirmation that truly focuses on the present—and the reality that now is a core concept—is: "I accept myself as I am and the world as it is." Such an affirmation delivers awareness and recognition about "what is" with acceptance and tolerance. It doesn't negate that you might have a call to action to take care of a sick child or handle a financial issue. Acceptance of "what is," though, comes with a deep understanding and insight of the moment, and solutions appear ever present.

For a special issue, you might choose from the following affirmations. Alternatively, develop your own affirmation, so that it resonates with you and truly strikes a chord of recognition.

Releasing the Past

- I hold no one responsible for all that has happened in the past. I am free and clear of all that has happened in the past.
- I remain present, unattached to memories of the past and outcomes of the future.

Self-Love

- I love myself unconditionally.
- I love and accept myself totally as I am.
- Everything that is highest and best, I automatically attract to myself.

Relationships

- Every time I renounce my judgment of others, I return to the source of self-empowerment within.
- As I am loving of others, I am loving of myself.
- I embrace the reality of everything as it is and all others as they are.

Health and Healing

- I enter the healing abode of my heart and release my unresolved feelings of fear, anger, blame, or shame.
- My body is light, my mind is at peace, and my heart is unconditionally open.
- I go to the source within that heals my body and mind.

Acceptance

- I have complete trust and faith in the mysterious workings of my higher self.
- I have entered the deepest state of letting go and am in a complete state of harmony and balance.
- I remain completely relaxed and receptive, regardless of the outcome or end result.

Staying on the Path

"During the springtime event, I had a major shift when I shared all the 'crap' I had been keeping inside. I had a major shift just learning and realizing that my life could be whatever I chose for myself. I have let myself wander off my path for these last few months due to my illness and lack of motivation. Now, I am reinforced with my commitment to yoga and meditation. I'm committed to my life and not letting my past conflict with my present. I have the 'Forgiveness and Acceptance' tattoos for a reason, and it's time I start abiding by those affirmations. I learned from the very first day to accept where my body was at physically in a pose and to let go of those judgments and negative thoughts.

"I don't know if I can put into words what this weekend meant to me. During Yogi Desai's second session on Saturday, when he was discussing the connection of our bodies and how they have the ability to heal themselves if we let them, and then we were lying on our backs, and he was speaking those affirmations about letting go of the past—my heart literally started hurting. The bottom right side of my heart started tightening up so much, I thought I was going to have to get out of the room right then. My breathing quickened so much that I felt like I was having a panic attack, but I kept thinking about the healing aspect of what we were doing, and I just let my body work out whatever it was going through. It was a few minutes and, all of a sudden, my heart stopped hurting, and I felt like my whole body was smiling. Even though there was no expression on my face and I wasn't even thinking about it in my mind, I knew that I had just healed my heart from all of my past experiences. My heart has figuratively hurt for my whole life, from the death of my parents to the way I was raised. I was able to physically feel that pain and that hurt and I was able to heal it and let it go! I cannot even explain to you what that felt like for me. It was like my soul was full of light, and I was so relieved and happy. It was absolutely amazing. My life has literally been changed because of it. I've spent so much time in therapy, and I've spent years trying to let go of all of the hatred, tragedy, and disap-

pointments from my life, but that exercise let me get
rid of all of that for good."

—A. Brennan, Pendleton, Oregon

Chapter 11

Practicing Yoga in Your Life

Yoga has passed the tipping point, the threshold where it's become a trendy practice that may result in increased flexibility and balance. Many mistakenly believe that yoga is just a stream of physical exercises. Postures form one piece of the yoga puzzle—but engaging in just that part of yoga without a deeper understanding can actually cause stress. In fact, the flood of yoga-studio openings across the country has been a huge boon to chiropractors, as unskilled practitioners teach postures without respect to the body and without mindfulness of mental agitations and disengagements.

The authentic yoga is a lifestyle of right choices that feed the body and soul, available and accessible to everyone at any moment and at every point in one's life, not just on a yoga mat. When the ego-mind is the performer of postures, your mind is actively engaged in self-criticism, comparing your performance with others and judging yourself and others. Your mind is agitated and engaged in internal conflict, even as your body is engaged in performing postures. The constant internal conflict causes your mind to be restless. Whenever you are mentally agitated and emotionally reactive to whatever you are facing at a given moment, you are in the posture of ego.

In defining what yoga is, Yogi Patanjali, the ancient authority, says, "Yoga means witnessing the mental modifications." *Yogas chitta vritti nirodhah.* (Yoga Sutras, 1:2). Whatever yoga form you practice, the highest priority and fundamental purpose is to eliminate mental agitations and emotional reactions. Performing yoga postures, you must change from an ego-driven posture—externally placing the body in a so-called yoga posture—and internally engage the mind, removing the ego-mind. No one has explained Patanjali's Yoga Sutra as the manual of yoga. All have translated it as philosophies instead of building it into one's practice as does I AM yoga. In I AM yoga, practice is motivated by integrative intention, the posture of consciousness that takes you into the Zero Stress Zone.

Understanding How to Use Yoga in Your Life

The I AM technique, as revealed in this book, has brought together some of the most ancient core values and principles that take the popular approach to the practice of yoga into a whole new dimension. It is designed not as a technique for the physical or mental discipline but to take you into the very innermost meaning and experience of the practice. You are not just learning how to practice yoga postures for increased physical benefits, such as losing weight, increasing flexibility, or learning a technique for temporary relaxation. Instead, you restore your connection to the consciousness by using yoga postures, breath work, and mental discipline as a medium to establish and awaken the heart and higher centers of integrated consciousness.

Thousands of people practice yoga in the form of an aerobic physical discipline; often, they go into the most complicated postures that focus on flexibility instead of experiencing a connection to the consciousness. I AM yoga reaches the inner depth and allows you to manage, monitor, and transform thoughts, feelings, and emotions that cause all physical problems or inhibitions.

The Edge

Yoga—like life—happens on the edge. When you enter a posture, notice what happens when you come to the edge where you cannot go any further. An argument with your spouse, a disagreement with your boss, or an irritation of being stuck in traffic may serve as a yoga posture. For most people on their first edge, they experience a subtle fight-or-flight reaction, and it turns into a battleground. This is an ego posture. Instead, when you dismantle your reaction by practicing *Pratyahara* and withdrawing your reaction to that edge, you turn the reaction into conscious, deliberate action. You relax and, by using a specific breath (such as the straw breath in the Quantum Breath Meditation), you convert the reactive pattern into a response. You accept yourself just the way you are and withdraw from self-criticism, fear, comparison of your performance with others, and judgment of others. At this point, you convert your ego-oriented reaction into conscious action.

Most people who perform yoga postures react to the edge, which represents a psychosomatic blockage. Every physical block has a psychological component. You cannot fight these psychosomatic blockages by breaking through them, because you cannot solve the problems of the ego-mind by the same ego-mind that created them. To transcend from ego-mind to a super-conscious state requires conscious withdrawal from the ego posture—letting go of fears, self-judgments, self-criticisms, and preprogrammed reactions—and entering a mindful connection to the posture of consciousness.

In I AM yoga, every time you arrive at an edge, you withdraw from your reaction and transition from *Hatha* yoga into *Raja* yoga, where you develop the ability to manage your own emotional reactions. Once you dismantle your reactive patterns on the edge, you dismantle your preprogrammed past.

The technique of transitioning through the psychosomatic edge on a yoga mat can apply to daily life. When you practice the posture of consciousness in your everyday life, you know how not to be edgy on the edge. People who have developed only yoga flexibility, temporary relaxation, or perfected postures are not prepared to face the mental, physical, and emotional challenges of life. They have not cultivated the consciousness, and their yoga skills fail to carry over into their personal, business, or family lives. For instance, when they have a conflict with a loved one or a boss, how will they solve the stress they've created? Will they do a yoga posture, stand on their head, and exclaim that the situation is resolved? The practice of the posture of consciousness yoga is extensively used as a medium for healing and transformation. Extensive research and study into the unique contribution of yogic science has revealed the validity and practical applications for restoring well-being.

Using the Past

The flow of time allows the past to orient you in the present. It is perfectly acceptable to use past experiences wisely as seeds for learning, developing, and preventing repetition of mistakes. However, if you are always trying to get back to conditions of the past or flee from them, you remove yourself from the natural flow and impede your own development. You get stuck in an energetic quicksand that suffocates all your power and buries your authentic self. You become disintegrated, overwhelmed, and crushed by life. Allowing yourself to align with the natural flow moves you closer to the deepest levels of integration. As that feeling occurs, there is an immediate sense of joy, of happiness, of oneness.

Relaxation and Stress

Often the word *relaxation* relates to the most surface-level application—used as an antidote to stress but completely different from the Zero Stress Zone. While watching television, drinking alcohol, reading, talking on the phone, and so forth. you experience a temporary sense of relaxation, but these choices can actually cause more stress. Through the I AM technique, you drop into the innermost core of your being, where all the stress and stress-related blocks created by the ego-mind on physical, mental, and emotional levels are released. As you move more toward the Zero Stress Zone, you reach deeper levels of integration, where all conflicting forces of body, mind, heart, and soul are brought into perfect balance, harmony, and unification. You connect with your true self—not the image your ego has created as your identity. As you embrace, recognize and accept your self, you are empowered. Your energies become vitalized as the channels and meridians of your body are opened and flowing. You see with more clarity, you understand with more insight, and you perform at the peak, feeling on top of the world! In this practice of the Posture of Consciousness, deliberate action moves you towards the non-doing integrative state of being. You drop into non-doing presence. In that state of content-less consciousness, you know who you are. When you empty your mind of reactive thoughts and feelings about yourself, what remains is

the essence of your being. You are non-reactive presence. You merge into Oneness in the Zero Stress Zone.

Yoga Nidra or Yogic Sleep

Another ancient form of meditation that takes you
into the deepest relaxation levels to reach the Zero
Stress Zone is Yoga Nidra. Representing the marriage
of science and spirit, Yoga Nidra takes you into a deep
state, beyond ordinary waking consciousness, in which
your brainwaves drop into alpha and theta states. You
completely shift out of identification with the body,
mind, and ego and naturally realign with spirit. You
effortlessly disengage from restrictive physical, mental,
and emotional patterns. In this state, you create a life
that is an expression of higher consciousness rather
than acquired conditioning. It is a simple healing
technique practiced by yogis for a millennium.

Yoga Nidra uses breath and focus on the Third
Eye to take you to a dimension where you erase hidden causes of stress. The literal translation of *nidra*
is "sleep." However, in the practice of Yoga Nidra,
it is a dynamic state, not the unconscious sleep of
slumber. It is practiced in a comfortable lying-down
position, known as *shavasana*. The facilitator guides
you through a series of breathing exercises and simple

instructions. In some methods, visual imagery is used or a scan of the body, where the mind momentarily focuses on a *marma* point, a point where concentrated life force energy is located, such as the shoulder, elbow, wrist, and so on. This occupies the mind with something mundane, preventing it from becoming involved in the usual mind chatter that absorbs ordinary consciousness and diminishes energy.

When you sleep, you automatically withdraw from the conflict-creating ego-mind, which superimposes many stressful patterns during waking hours. Problems disappear until you awake back to them. In normal sleep, your inborn survival level restores the body's balance: the autonomic nervous system. However, sleep does not eliminate the stressful patterns hidden in unconscious habit patterns. Yogic sleep is a quantum leap from survival-level ordinary sleep to an evolutionary level of transformation. You not only receive the restful restorative experiences, as in nighttime sleep, but you can go deeper, where you dismantle stress-producing patterns from the core. No matter how much regular sleep you get, you will achieve a state of rest but will never reach enlightenment. Yoga Nidra opens the door to dismantling self-destructive habit patterns—such as overeating, alcoholism, drug addiction, or tranquilizers—at the very source, leading to an internal shift connecting to your inner being.

How does this Yoga Nidra state create a shift within you? During the daytime, you operate in beta brain waves, often caught in emotional conflicts causing reactions that engage attention and energy in self-sabotaging ways. This can be changed only when you accept yourself just as you are and withdraw from all forms of blame or shame that keep you mentally and emotionally disturbed. Yoga Nidra takes you temporarily to the state of total acceptance of everything as it is.

Most people who try to eliminate self-destructive patterns almost invariably become frustrated about their own behaviors. Someone suffering from obesity begins with such a wounded self-image that whatever he or she adopts as an approach to losing weight is tied in with self-rejection and guilty feelings. These act as motivation to change addiction and habits, but the stress pattern at the core of the addiction is sustained, while the person tries to eliminate the bad habit. Even if people are successful in eliminating their addictions, the stress that remains unaddressed will manifest through another negative pattern. Stress is the cause. Addictions are the effects, the surface symptoms.

People are helpless victims of their own unconscious habit patterns.

To remove the cause, one typically eliminates stress patterns from the source. If you stop drinking or smoking, you may suddenly have problems with your relationships or your work. The stress that was unresolved got diverted into other patterns, so it comes back in the form of another symptom. The uniqueness of Yoga Nidra—like the Quantum Breath Meditation—is that it is designed to dismantle the essential cause of stress.

Within a short time, you are submerged in the alpha state, where brain rhythms drop into the silent space within. Once your body is relaxed and your mind is calm, all energies are focused on the Third Eye, the inner sanctuary located between the eyebrows. Simultaneously, you access the logical left brain and the intuitive, insightful right brain. This naturally and effortlessly brings you into integration, where you experience deep relaxation yet remain aware and conscious.

Modern science now reinforces what yogis discovered thousands of years ago: that focusing on the Third Eye activates hormones located in the pineal gland in the center of the brain. These hormones, melatonin and serotonin, are powerful agents to retard premature aging, reduce stress, induce more restful sleep, boost the immune system, and promote healing. In normal sleep, you transition from the self-conscious waking state to the subconscious sleep state. In Yoga Nidra, you transition from waking to a superconscious state. While ordinary sleep may renew the body and refresh the mind, it cannot alter your unconscious programming. Yoga Nidra goes beyond, to eliminate the unconscious obstructions that keep you from connecting to the source from which your inborn potential may be actualized.

Many therapists, psychologists, healthcare professionals, life coaches, and yoga teachers have found this system to be an extraordinary extension to the services they provide.

What's Karma Got to Do With It?

You are born in this life to continue the process of evolving to your highest divine potential. The soul moves from lifetime to lifetime, journeying through birth and death and carrying out its evolutionary experiences. The birth of the body is not the beginning of the journey; there is life before birth. Nor is death the end; it is just another beginning. The soul takes a body in order to fulfill its unresolved experiences of past lifetimes. People are born with different personalities, psychological conditions, and environments that are in direct harmony for what the soul is seeking. The soul creates the appropriate conditions for evolution through the fulfillment of desires.

Last night, when you fell asleep, many tasks were left unresolved, to be completed the next day. So it is with lifetimes. At death, the soul discards the body, because it is no longer an appropriate vehicle to continue with its evolutionary journey. It picks a new body and continues where it stopped. If there was no life before, where did it come from? There is no explanation. Siblings born of the same parents, brought up in the same environment and in the same way, have totally distinct personalities. What you are carrying with you, in the form of karmic patterns, personality, and behavior patterns, has been with you since time immemorial with the journey of your soul.

Karma and reincarnation cannot be separated. They are intimately related. The soul is impersonal. Everything you think you are as a personality or karma never touches the soul. No matter what crimes you as the personality perform, the soul is never touched. The soul is forever pure. No matter how many clouds or weather patterns cover the sun, the sun never gets blemished. Similarly, karma can never blemish the soul. You just have passing experiences. Therefore, everyone can realize divine potential and be enlightened. Why don't you? You identify with who you are not.

The power and authority of the soul are taken away when you believe you can only be punished for the wrongs you have done. This form of belief system in religious circles creates fear, preventing you from taking charge of your own enlightenment. Fear impairs your capacity to disengage from your own karmic blocks to realize the divine being that you are. According to many religious beliefs, there is no way to return to the soul until all the punishment has been performed and until the last judgment day.

If you cannot accept the doctrine of reincarnation, then you must accept life as accidental. You have to believe in luck, accidents, and miracles. Nothing happens in this world without a cause. This is the Universal Law of Cause and Effect. In this current lifetime, you experience the effects of what you caused somewhere in your past; you call this karma. The purpose of I AM Yoga is to recognize that what you are experiencing is a direct result of what you have caused that you don't remember causing. When you experience pain, suffering, ecstasy, or fulfillment, you experience the effects of the cause that is your karma.

In the Bible, this can be likened to the story of the
Garden of Eden. In the journey of the soul, it assumes
individuality and tries to find on its own what it already
had in the domain of the Father, God. The soul separates from the original source and, with an individual
sense of "I am," begins to search for oneness.

In the Garden of Eden, Adam and Eve were one—
but when they ate the fruit of the tree of good and evil,
by choosing one, they became two. Prior to becoming
"I am," you are in the Garden of Eden, which is heaven
or oneness with God. Now, you are outside the Garden
of Eden. You know what is needed to return: purity and
impersonal unity. Everything added after the phrase
"I am" is adopted and acquired. It is not original and
is conditioned by society, culture, belief systems, and
personal bias, which distort the perception of everything that comes through it.

To continue to evolve, you need to realize that your
experience of life is your own creation. Every time you
fear something, resist someone, or avoid something,
you ignore an opportunity to burn the deed of karma
that you caused at some time. Once you choose for
or against what is present, you create karma. If you
remain the silent witness, the observer—"Thy will be
done, not mine"—you are no longer choosing. When

you allow and accept the interplay of polarity, of opposites, you return to unity.

There is a subtle memory that continues to live beyond the physical body and carries with it all the unresolved past. Souls attract each other to play out their karma. In this way, karma assumes a balancing process, much of it prompted unconsciously. You are driven towards those situations and encounters where the imbalance can be resolved—provided that you are aware. You attract relationships to help see those things that you haven't yet chosen to see. Then, when the lessons come, you blame the other for the unhappiness, sorrow, or suffering. There is no unhappiness, there is no suffering, there is only balancing. It is karma working its way out.

To work out your karma, let go of whatever emotions and conflicts come up. Let it be and don't take it personally. The part that is taking it personally is the karma. If *you* don't take it personally, the karma that was taking it personally is resolved. If there is nothing to be resolved, there is only unity. If there is nothing to be resolved, there is no karma.

The ancient sages used the sport of archery to explain the workings of karma. There are three kinds of arrows:

1. Arrows in the quiver. Latent stored *samskaras* or impressions in the unconscious. These are predispositions and habit patterns waiting for an opportunity to come into action.

2. Arrows in hand. These are the ones you presently have a choice about shooting. Being aware of your motives, the nature of your desires, attractions, and repulsions, you can shoot by choice rather than unconsciously.

3. Arrows in the air. These are the actions that are playing themselves out. These are thoughts, actions, and words that are already in motion. They will bring consequences or fruit. These need to be accepted; you should not beat yourself up over them, which creates more karma. You just move forward from here.

As you become more conscious, you shoot from choice, not habit or reactive behaviors. As your aim improves, the outcome is better. When you don't know where to aim, it is difficult to know what to shoot at, so you find that you shoot at every like, dislike, fear, or desire that comes into your life. Finding a target or an intention means you have something to choose to aim at. If you choose peace, your choices will be made to bring you closer to that target.

The greater part of karma has to do with why you do the action and who is to receive the benefit of the action. It can come to me. It can be offered to others. It can be offered to God. Whenever there is attachment to the end result, it breeds more karma, usually in the form of wanting more and more. When the motivation is to serve others and not only yourself, then you are free of the attachments.

Learning Non-Reaction

"I can fully feel the benefits inside my body, energetically rather than mentally. Relaxation is one of the master keys that Gurudev has given to me, whether this relaxation is used in Yoga Nidra (to allow me to bring intention into the subconscious mind), during yoga to help me with my asana practice, or as a way of opening the natural flow of *Prana* in my body. The experiences have given me a tool, a relaxation remedy, that I use on a daily basis. Modern life is full of small, medium, and major stressors. When something irritates me, I can more easily feel it physically, then move to relaxation and let the stress and the negative impact of it pass on by. What a gift.

"Relaxing and living in the present moment definitely improve my relationships. I am more accepting of what other people do and say and more open to a wider range of possible directions. I am still learning, of course. In fact, every interaction with another human becomes an opportunity for both celebration and personal growth. I really appreciate that.

"Gurudev teaches us so many things. One of the foundations of his teachings relates to awareness about our own reactions. Every single day, I have an opportunity to work on this one, with a comment from a friend or relative or an unexpected event that is not what I had hoped for. More than ever, I catch myself early on, as I begin to react. Sometimes, I still have reactions. The difference is that I can watch the reaction and acknowledge it for what it is. I no longer get caught up in the energy and continue on by abusing myself or others with negative comments. I can settle in and find that space within myself, where I recognize the transitory nature of the event or comment and am able to move ahead without getting caught up in the story. This is huge! How much of my precious energy, my *Prana*, and my time are now saved. Ironically, this presence of mind sometimes stirs up reaction in the person or people that I deal with. Clearly, the teachings can continue to move outward!

—Bill Eager, Internet Expert and Yoga Teacher, Denver, Colorado

Chapter 12

Energetic Transmission for Connecting to the Power of Presence Within

For Healing Yourself

The truth of these Integrated Amrit Method (I AM) practices is received directly through the medium of energetic transmission through the presence of a master. The medium of energetic synchronicity is effectively received by the combined practice of energetic transmission and personal practice, opening the door for you to enter into harmonious interaction with the *Pranic* energy field within. Once you live in harmony with the energy field of polarity, it is reflected in every interaction you have—with life's situations, challenges, and relationships—to highly accelerate your spiritual progress into another dimension.

Energetic transmission is already occurring in the dimension of words that you are reading in this book. There is a resonance to the words that carries a vibrational frequency. You receive the meanings of the words conceptually, but you can also receive them energetically. If you are sensitive and open—without resistance and tension—you feel their quantum transmission. When you're in a relaxed mood in an alpha brainwave state, you have dropped from the thinking level to the energetic feeling level. Once you have entered that state, you are in synergy with your energy field, and there is a felt shift in your perception. When words of truth are heard, they reach to the innermost core of knowing and create a paradigm shift, a burst of light and knowledge that gets metabolized in your body and your being. Words are coming through the mind, but you hear directly through your energy body.

What Is the Anatomy of Transformative Learning?
A Two-Way Exchange

Transmission is not a one-way process. The energetic transmission that creates a quantum leap in your personal growth, healing, and transformation happens only when you are ready and open to enter into the synchronicity of the energy field, where transmission spontaneously takes place. When the master enters into the energy field, the student who is relaxed can spontaneously receive the *shaktipot,* the connection. When that happens, the student must continually nurture the seed of energetic transmission to create a sustainable container.

In the energy field of the Zero Stress Zone, the door opens for you to enter into the synchronicity with the presence of the master. When a student is ready, the teacher appears; when the disciple is ready, the guru appears. But this is not entirely true. The truth is that, when the disciple is ready, the guru is recognized. This energetic transmission is a symbiotic interplay in which you enter into oneness at a cosmic energetic level.

As you get illuminated, you become the carrier of the light. When the healer enters the all-embracing dimension of awareness, the luminous presence begins to spread and extend like a flower blooming and transmitting a fragrance. The flower doesn't have to push the fragrance on passersby to prove it has the fragrance. Once you are awakened, the light spreads wherever you go. You become the carrier and the emissary of the light.

Everyone has at one time or another experienced energetic transmission on a negative level, where some person who is emotionally frustrated or angry enters a room and almost immediately everyone senses the change in the energy field. It's as if the life is sucked out of the room. The negative field radiates from this individual and creates a noticeably unpleasant shift for everyone. But it is the rare experience for someone to experience a powerful energetic transmission from a master force. It is extraordinary to witness the impact of someone who has the facility to drop into the cosmic energy field and erase all the boundaries and limitations of the ego-mind. The master can easily drop into the integrated Zero Stress Zone, creating his own field and radiating that to everyone. Those who are ready and open instantly merge through the impersonal energetic resonance. On this level, the spiritual teachings that cannot be imparted conceptually, intellectually, or mentally can be transmitted experientially and energetically.

The Portal to Connect with the Cosmic Energy Field Can Be Effortless

In India, this is a most ancient tradition that has developed a whole new channel of communion, often expressed as having trust and faith in God or in a guru. Once you understand this mystical dimension of energetic transmission, you may learn how to purify your body, your mind, and your heart to develop that opening.

Without having to struggle or work for many years to achieve this integrated state, you can receive it through this guru-disciple relationship, which gives you direct access and experience. Once you know this to be real, your faith in the unknown dimension arises spontaneously and naturally.

When you first receive the transmission, you're riding on the master's energy, but as you practice the techniques, you connect with the same energy consciousness on your own. Once you connect with the power of the source within, you feel a new sense of self-confidence and integrity that is no longer asking for love, approval, or recognition. This connection is to the love and light of the guru within. The energetic teachings of the guru outside connect and actualize the guru within, which naturally turns into faith, trust, and love for the guru. Some who read the philosophy about the guru-disciple relationship cannot understand the inner dimension. Only a true disciple, who has awakened the guru within through the teachings of the external guru, can appreciate this relationship and continue to grow.

The connection to the spirit within becomes so powerfully magnetic that everything you are looking for—that could never be achieved previously—happens spontaneously. Everything that you were striving for, struggling to get, and failing to receive now begins to come to you without asking, demanding, controlling, or causing. When you are one with the cosmic ocean of energy, the whole universe converges blessings upon you.

On an internal level, you ask for nothing, and it is all given. You demand nothing, and everything is fulfilled from the dimension of grace. When you continue to practice the techniques, you establish that state of consciousness connecting to the infinite source of power, strength, courage, and confidence.

In this transported dimension, the meek are the blessed. "The meek shall inherit the earth," says the Bible. "Meek" means humble. This is the fourth dimension. It is a non-linear, non-mental, time-transcendent dimension. The light that you see in the guru is a reflection of the light that you have connected to within yourself. That is why it is said "It takes a thief to catch a thief." It takes an enlightened being to recognize one.

Once you open to the energetic receptivity, you can enter this dimension any time you choose. Transported by the energy, you enter a state of *Samadhi* or bliss. The ego-mind dies, and you are reincarnated into the zone, where everything happens from an effortless dimension. It's the way the saints and realized masters live. They have a connection. They don't judge anyone or feel judged by anyone.

The more often you meditate, you naturally come into that state of flow where you are not forcing anything. It becomes an ecstatic way of life. The outer world becomes an illusion that you easily see through. You look at a person and see what he or she is going through, and you have compassion. There will be no anger or any emotion, just compassion. When you live in the *Prana*, that's where you enter. Everything that you see in that dimension goes through your higher consciousness, not your mind. You're not practicing psychic healing, but your very presence becomes healing. In this state, your mind will not understand and will call the experience "weird" or "a miracle" or "an accident." But it is a direct energetic transmission from the masters and needs to be nurtured consciously through practice. In this way, you become the light, the connection to God.

A Saint-Like Experience

"How I came to find Gurudev was very interesting. The first time I ever studied with Gurudev. I went to Akron. Spent a week or so doing yoga *nidra* and meditation. Prior to that, my practice was mostly physical. But yet I was drawn to him and his picture. I kept seeing his picture seemingly everywhere. So I looked him up and saw he was going to be in the area, so I traveled there.

"The last day—beautiful, wonderful, relaxing experience. To be honest, I was sitting in the back and leaning back on my hands. And he said, 'I'm going to show you something. Relax and watch.' He wasn't telling us what he was going to do. He went into a meditative state. I wasn't meditating. I was fully aware and conscious. I was daydreaming, thinking about my children. Kind of zoning out. I happened to glance up at Gurudev, and I noticed the people in front of me were somehow transparent. I could see through them. That was the first thing that happened. My mind was kind of going 'Okay, what's happening here?' But part of me was 'Oh, this is cool. No worries.' I looked up at him, and it seemed as if people were dissolving around me. People were becoming more and more transparent. As he was doing his breath and he stopped the breath, it seemed like particles of light were everywhere, like little stars or sunshine, and it seemed that they were surrounding me. And I was surrounded by this light. I felt like I was extremely...I have no words for it, except I felt I was in the presence of God.

"And I was there for I don't know how long. I had no body. No sense of time. Nothing, other than this incredible sensation of happiness. Bliss and comfort. But there was also a part of me that was still there, that was going 'What's going on? What's happening here?' It was almost like I was two different people. I was one person where I was, and it was everything as it should be; another was going 'Wait a minute,' but that voice was so far behind me. I don't know how long I was in that space. But when I came back from this experience, I looked down at my body, and I was moving, which to me was very unusual. I looked, and my arms were moving, and I wasn't moving my arms. My mind was saying 'You shouldn't do that.' People will look and think I was having an epileptic seizure or something because my arms were twitching. And part of me was saying it's okay, let it happen.

"That happened for a while. It wasn't an entirely pleasant sensation. It was as if I had put my finger in an electric socket and that sensation like I was being shocked. And I was seeing spots, like my eyes had been exposed to a bright, bright light. Like you'd looked at a light bulb or sunshine. And I thought that was curious, because no one had taken a picture or shined a light.

"The most amazing thing happened to me following that, and it lasted for about eight weeks or so. Life was completely without effort. Everything that came to mind that I wanted or needed immediately came to me. It was uncanny. And I didn't have to verbalize. It was incredible. For instance, I was at the strip center, and I had left my bank card in the car. I got to Stan's Market, and I needed $20, and I didn't have the money to pay. I was rifling through my purse looking for my bank card. And I was thinking 'I gotta have $20.' And the man behind me said 'Here, do you need $20?' and he handed it to me. It sounds so strange, but that was not uncommon. Things were immediately, spontaneously given to me without verbalizing.

"The other thing that happened is that complete strangers were drawn to me. I would turn around, and people would be talking to me about their innermost personal experiences. There were people who would tell me they had been lying. They'd been struggling with family members. They wouldn't even introduce themselves. They would just start talking to me. It wasn't me answering. I could see myself speaking, but I wasn't saying it. It was coming out of me. I had people who were seeking comfort from horrific experiences. Deaths that they had witnessed. Imprisonment. All sorts of interesting things. Sometimes people coming up and just spontaneously hugging me. This will sound very unusual, but I felt connected not only to people. I would see someone, and I *knew* what he or she needed. Not only people but animals, plants. I seemed to be able to understand the garden and what it needed but not in a verbal way, not in words...

"It was the most beautiful experience to live in that. I have a Catholic, Christian upbringing, and the kingdom of heaven is here. There is no heaven over there. You die, and you have an admission to heaven. Heaven is right here everywhere. It is with all of us. I

had an overwhelming understanding of that....I immediately lost my fear...of others...I had no fear of death.
I feel like, from that experience, I kind of experienced
death while being alive and conscious. I know what
that is. This is where I'm going. This is who I am. Everything was vibrant. My vision changed. Colors were
brighter. People were brighter. It's very difficult to put
into words, because I don't have the vocabulary to
describe the sensations that occurred.

"I found it amazing there were no introductions
necessary. No names exchanged. It was just spontaneous. My husband called it 'A Trish Moment.'

"I was doing nothing. I was non-doing. Sometimes,
in the past, I made an effort to meditate and that
was of the mind. For me, personally, I think it took
me coming into it in a daydreaming state. I had never
experienced anything like that. I was not paying any
attention with the mind. I was lost. Zoning out. And
it's a very beautiful experience."

—Trish, Philadelphia, Pennsylvania

Chapter 13

Living in the Zero Stress Zone

When you practice, you see a miraculous shift. Fears, anxieties, angers, and insecurities are released, and you see with greater clarity. Ego blindness is lifted. As you explore this dimension—and experience these miracles—you develop trust and faith, allowing you to take a quantum leap. You tune into creative realms where you may feel as if you have received divine protection or guidance.

Only when you go beyond struggle, strife, conflicts, and emotional episodes can you access the zone. Once you are engaged in the zone, which is *a causal,* you create a space for a whole new sacred domain to take over whatever you are doing. A causal means you don't have to cause something for the effect to happen. When you are free from controlling, forcing, demanding, expecting, and pushing, all that you want comes to you, just as you need it and as much of it as you need. When you practice being in the zone, you can act from beyond fear and insecurity. In this way, your insight, intuition, and creativity bloom, and you see solutions where before you saw only problems.

Commitment

At past workshops, disciples would be given the opportunity to learn the Quantum Breath Meditation technique only if they signed a commitment to practice it twice a day. The request was very precise, and it was not negotiable. Those who refused to sign the agreement were asked to leave. There was no judgment or questions asked, they were just not given the Integrated Amrit Method (I AM) technique. For the more advanced Quantum Breath Meditation, this requirement is still imposed.

The purpose of the contract is to instill the value and power of the meditation technique. You can have thousands of perfect tools in your toolbox, but if you never use any of them, nothing will ever be accomplished. Nothing will be built. It is the same with the I AM techniques. If you do not commit to using them regularly, you cannot reach the Zero Stress Zone, and you may never experience the magic of life as an effortless flow.

Explored, practiced, and experienced by thousands, the Quantum Breath Meditation has consistently proven to be effective and easy to adopt. It allows even the novice practitioner to enter into the deepest levels.

The Real Path

When you establish a routine of practice and make time for it—with the same behavioral conditioning that you use when you wake up and brush your teeth in the morning—you establish a deeper connection with your core being, your inner self. Commitment allows you to overcome all the barriers that keep you from realizing your highest potential, holding you back from being in the light of ultimate consciousness. When you take to the path of transformation—if it is the real path—it requires seeing everything that you have been avoiding, fearing, or denying. That is the path.

Pain Is Evitable; Suffering Is Optional

The moment you make a commitment, occasions will arise for you to resist following through. But that does not mean life should be lived without direction, without any rudder. Life has to be guided with intention; that is the willful path. When you walk that path, you will be afraid; you will experience pain and the desire to run from it, suppress it, or justify why you don't have to face it or your life the way it is. If you want to be comfortable, don't make commitments! Everything that has been keeping you from realizing your potential will come up, and you will have to deny all those distractions, saying, "No, I'm going to stand in my center, in my core, in my being."

Commitment is about consciously carving the path and creating what you are. Live from the possibility that commitment is not an obligation but a privilege. It is not about productivity; it's about something that happens inside you, which is what gives it significance.

The Honeymoon Is Just the Beginning

In a marriage, your life is not what happens on the day of the honeymoon; it's what you create after the honeymoon because of your commitment. The honeymoon is just the beginning. If there is no commitment to the intention of who you are in the relationship, the relationship just falls apart within a very short time.

What you want is not something that happens by the virtue of external events coming together but by the virtue of your willingness to continue to let it happen with your commitment. The mind will come up with many different reasons to avoid *your commitment*, but that is habitual—the mechanical robotic part of your highly conditioned mind and persona. For instance, you commit to being on time, and the mind says, "Oh, I have an important phone call to make." That's what is bound to happen, which is why you are making a commitment.

What has been in charge of your life are your habits, concepts, and beliefs. You have been brainwashed, and now you have to wash it out, so that who you really are can begin to emerge. The commitment is to access the You that has been hiding. In spite of the fear, you must align again and again with commitment, instead of getting entrenched in the fear. If you make a commitment to your chosen intention and give your life to it, you are choosing to realign with what is.

Chapter 14

Moving from Aging to Timeless Consciousness

The Difference You Make

These ancient mystical teachings are the gift of truth received from a lineage of beings who were able to reach the highest level of cosmic consciousness. They are not gathered by the people who received them and expanded them conceptually, intellectually, logically, or rationally with logical thinking. Instead, they are wisdom received directly, non-mentally, from having reached the innermost core of stillness within. It is *senatan dharma* or eternal truth. It represents what Christ says: "Be still and know that I am God." These seers reached the level of such complete stillness in the non-doing power of presence. What came through them was direct teachings from the higher power called God, which resides within you.

When you connect to the light within, you have a powerful ability to spread that light. World peace is not the function of one person. It cannot be achieved unless each person learns how to transcend the self-image that lives in perpetual conflict, a conflict that is exacerbated by reaction to other people's perpetual conflicts with their self-images. By releasing the self-image and transcending the karmic body, you move effortlessly from darkness to light, and you see the truth. You glow with the knowledge of potential.

Being present with what is allows you to see exactly what is going on around you: reality. You are in tune with natural laws, the flux of constant change. You ebb with the tides and bend with the winds. This means no more and no less. It gives freedom from fixed ideas of what has to be. Your identity is no longer dependent on outside experiences but is naturally free-flowing from your inner self. You do not cling to any one moment; rather, you relish that moment for what it is. If you strive for the golden coin of happiness based on yesterday and tomorrow, you miss the treasure of today.

Question Yourself

Become aware. Ask yourself and explore, "How does my experience of these external events represent my own personal reaction to them?" "How can I regain clarity and objectivity that can truly solve both personal and global issues that I am facing?" Before you expect external shifts in the world, let inner shifts remain at the core.

Every crisis contains a lesson to learn to reshape and transcend past conditioning. Every event that appears painful or hurtful holds a message that can empower you to transform the world you live in. When you avoid the experience of hurt and pain, you invariably miss the message. If you miss this opportunity, you miss the possibility for a change in global consciousness. When seemingly unpleasant events occur in life, instead of reacting with fear or grief, ask yourself: "What do I need to learn from this experience?"

Just as the forest is made up of trees, the world is made up of individuals. Only individuals have the possibility to influence and prevent tragic events from reoccurring through a personal shift in consciousness. Consciousness means finding the middle path, where you are free from the primal drives of anger, fear, retaliation, and the belief that overcoming an external enemy will give you internal resolution. The middle path transcends the duality of extremism and opposites. It sees with the light of clarity, objectivity, and understanding.

Find that place within yourself, and you will create the right response and the right action. When the critical balance shifts towards more individuals living this way, the hundredth-monkey effect will bring about a change in global consciousness. (The *hundredth monkey* is a phenomenon in which a new behavior or idea is claimed to spread rapidly by unexplained or even supernatural means, from one group to all related groups, once a critical number of members of one group exhibit the new behavior or acknowledge the new idea.) It all begins and ends with each person.

Success and Freedom

In today's culture, people haven't yet realized the value of what they do to themselves in the process of achieving success or making dreams come true. The meaning of success in our society is created by a collective unconscious, in which success is perceived as something you make happen externally. But it happens at the cost of what you do to yourself internally. You need to find the passage back to the source within.

Simplicity unclutters your life and your mind. You respond to life just as it is in each moment, seeking no more. You may believe that such a life would be very dull. The fact is that life is a perpetual adventure when you are attentive to what is happening inside and around you. When you feel no need to suppress, deny, hold onto, or fight with life, you enjoy its simple sweetness as you let go more and more of illusory expectations. There is no greater satisfaction than the ability to be absorbed in basic activities: eating a balanced, nourishing meal with gratitude, with full attention to its flavors, textures, and smells; walking in nature, aware of the aroma of fresh earth and the feel of the breeze in one's hair; or listening openly and attentively to a loved one. When you experience life with such childlike freshness, then life reveals its joys, wonder, and mysteries, and your deepest longings are fulfilled.

Problems will come. But when you live with awareness, every problem reveals its own solution. You develop the Midas touch that converts base metal into gold. Challenges become opportunities. Pain changes into freedom from pain. This is the alchemy of life.

As you move toward your inner Source, your internal knowing guides you to the next step on the path. You receive the higher calling of your spirit to live the truths of love, beauty, peace, service, and full creative expression. And you are released from all suffering. You are finally free to live.

About Gurudev Amrit Desai

Gurudev Shri Amritji (Yogi Amrit Desai) is an interna-
tionally recognized authority on yoga and holistic living.
Widely acknowledged for carrying the authentic voice of
yoga to the world, he has been honored both in the United
States and abroad. Some of his distinguished titles include
Doctor of Yoga, Jagadacharya (Universal Teacher), and the
rare Vishwa Yoga Ratna, awarded by the President of India.
Gurudev Amrit Desai began teaching yoga in 1960, making
him one of the earliest pioneers of yoga in the West. Following a profound life-transforming Kundalini awakening, he
developed a methodology that altered the popular notion
of yoga as a physical discipline and reintroduced a spiritual
dimension to the practice of Hatha Yoga. He named this
approach Kripalu Yoga: Meditation in Motion, in honor
of his guru, Swami Kripalvanandji. The yoga society Yogi
Desai founded eventually grew to become Kripalu Center
for Yoga and Health, one of the largest centers of its kind in
America. The methodology he developed has evolved into
the Amrit Method, which he continues to refine at the Amrit
Yoga Institute, the thriving Yoga and Ayurveda Center in
Salt Springs, Florida. Today, his approach is practiced by
thousands around the world, with certified teachers in 37
countries.

Amrit Yoga Institute
23855 NE County Rd 314
Salt Springs, FL 32134
352-685-3001
https://amrityoga.org/
http://www.yogiamritdesai.com/

For Products, Books, CDs
https://iam.yoga/

https://www.facebook.com/YogiAmritDesai/
https://www.facebook.com/amrityogainstitute/

About Peggy Sealfon

Peggy Sealfon is a Personal Development Coach, Author, Motivational Speaker and owns Stonewater Studio, a natural way to health and wellness. Certified in Amrit Yoga and Yoga Nidra, she is also trained in functional medicine, functional nutrition, life coaching, modern psychology (NLP), energy medicine, and the neurosciences. Her best-selling book is ***Escape From Anxiety: Supercharge Your Life With Powerful Strategies From A to Z.*** She is co-author of ***The Change: Insights Into Self Empowerment*** (with Jim Britt, Tony Robbins's first mentor, and others). She resides in Naples, Florida.

Contact Info:
http://www.PeggySealfon.com
http://StonewaterStudio.com
https://www.facebook.com/
        peggysealfon.personaldevelopmentcoach/
https://twitter.com/StonewaterSt
https://www.linkedin.com/in/peggysealfon
Peggy@PeggySealfon.com
239.821.2266

StonewaterStudio.com

CPSIA information can be obtained
at www.ICGtesting.com
Printed in the USA
FFHW010642140319
51031314-56455FF